DATE DUE			

Science Policy
from Ford to Reagan

Science Policy from Ford to Reagan
Change and Continuity

Claude E. Barfield

American Enterprise Institute for Public Policy Research
Washington and London

Claude E. Barfield was a visiting fellow at the American Enterprise Institute in 1981 and served as co–staff director of the President's Commission for a National Agenda for the Eighties from 1979 to 1981.

Library of Congress Cataloging in Publication Data

Barfield, Claude E.
  Science policy from Ford to Reagan.

  (AEI studies ; 375)
  1. Science and state—United States. 2. Technology and state—United States. 3. Federal aid to research—United States. I. Title. II. Series.
  Q127.U6B27   1982   353.0085'5   82—16354
  ISBN 0-8447-3495-0
  ISBN 0-8447-3494-2 pbk.

AEI Studies 375

Printed in the United States of America

Contents

Foreword

The United States is recognized as a leader in scientific and technological progress. One of the major reasons for this achievement has been the wide support, both public and private, of research and development activities. Claude E. Barfield, a visiting fellow at the American Enterprise Institute, examines the research and development strategies of the Ford, Carter, and Reagan administrations. The author studies the policies of the three administrations by describing and analyzing both change and continuity in the principles and actual operations of the federal science support system.

Dr. Barfield's final chapter consists of a comprehensive summary and a group of policy recommendations. His proposals are thoughtful and feasible because they attempt to anticipate emerging issues and problems for government-sponsored research and development. His suggestions build upon areas of consensus that have evolved during the past three administrations and are tailored to fit the tight fiscal conditions that are likely to remain for the foreseeable future.

The broadest recommendation the author makes is that the primary concern of the White House and Congress should be directed toward the long-term, basic research elements in the research and development budget. This proposal follows from the fact that the private sector will not support this research at an adequate level for several reasons: because the private reward accruing to firms tends to be a small portion of the return received by society as a whole; because of the risk and uncertainty associated with such research; and because, in most cases, there is the need for sizable, long-term investment. It is appropriate for the federal government to act to ensure an adequate level of spending for research to advance general scientific knowledge.

Dr. Barfield admits that there are no exact criteria for establishing the adequacy of the federal basic research budget. Government support must, then, be determined using relatively arbitrary rules. He adds that funding decisions should have a basis in the experience of past programs and should uphold the conviction that scientific progress is dependent on steady and reliable support, free from abrupt swings and redirections.

Predictability is just as important as stability in ensuring the continuing health of basic scientific research. For this reason, major publications that outline research priorities, such as the annual report of the National Science Board, should be revised so that they lay out recommendations over at least a five-year period. The White House, after evaluating these recommendations, should describe and update the administration's long-range plans for increasing, maintaining, or decreasing particular areas of research funding.

The author notes that the current administration would be well advised to undertake a full-scale review of the organization of federal science and technology programs with the goal of recommending an optimum, workable structure to meet current pressures and future challenges. Such a review would be timely because past and current proposals to consolidate some technological agencies and disband others have raised a number of unanswered questions.

The author recognized that a collection of factors argued for a reexamination of the federal science and technology support system. He has provided his answer to this challenge with this comprehensive review.

WILLIAM J. BAROODY, JR.
President
American Enterprise Institute

Preface

The sweeping changes in domestic and social policy set in motion by the Reagan administration have important counterparts in science and technology policy. In February 1981, well before the full dimensions of these policy shifts were evident, a respected writer for the magazine *Chemical and Engineering News* stated:

> The 1980s already are turning out to be a decade of shocks to America's vaunted technological system. From university departments to the boardrooms of big and small businesses, traditional assumptions are being rent by doubt. . . . A shift in the way of looking at the world certainly is coming in with the neoconservative Reagan administration, and science and technology policy is bound to be affected. Some say, in fact, that the old rule book on the funding of science and technology might as well be tossed out with yesterday's newspaper.[1]

Almost a year later, in January 1982, President Reagan's science adviser, George A. Keyworth, underscored the magazine's prediction when he addressed the American Association for the Advancement of Science (AAAS): he said it was "clear that today's federal role in science and technology must be different from that which has prevailed since World War II. A changing world as well as changing national goals call for changes in science policy."[2]

There are a number of significant redirections in science policy implemented by the Reagan administration to illustrate Keyworth's theme:

• The roles of the federal government and the private sector have been more sharply delineated, and the line beyond which the federal government should not go has been drawn far back toward the basic research end of the research and development (R & D) spectrum. This

1. Will Lepkowsky, "Reshaping Ahead for U.S. Science Policy," *Chemical and Engineering News*, February 23, 1981, p. 22.

2. George A. Keyworth, director, Office of Science and Technology Policy, address delivered before the American Association for the Advancement of Science, Washington, D.C., January 3, 1982.

has resulted in a drastic curtailment of federal support for demonstration and commercialization projects, particularly in the field of energy.

• Science projects are being more directly evaluated in relation to the administration's perception of their contribution to long-term productivity and economic growth. This policy has produced increased priority for the so-called hard sciences—physics, chemistry, biology, basic engineering—and decreased support for the soft, or social, sciences.

• The federal government will use only indirect incentives—tax and budget reductions, regulatory reform—to spur industrial innovation. Direct government intervention programs undertaken by the Carter administration—such as joint government-industry generic technology centers and joint government-industry programs of basic research on automobiles and the internal combustion engine—have been dismantled.

• R & D priorities have been shifted dramatically. Defense R & D accounts for more than 60 percent of total federal R & D expenditures in fiscal 1983. Nuclear programs account for 66 percent of the total energy R & D.

Although changes in approach and priorities brought about by the Reagan administration were undoubtedly far reaching, it would be a mistake to focus solely on discontinuity. There also emerged substantial continuity with the post–World War II consensus regarding the importance of science to national economic growth and to the achievement of domestic and national security goals. Thus, in the same speech to the AAAS in January 1982, Keyworth stated:

> The Reagan administration places great value on our country's scientific and technological strength. Supporting science is a necessity for all great nations, and certainly for the United States. Success in achieving virtually all of our national goals for the 1980s—more vigorous economic growth, enhanced national security, a stronger competitive position in world markets, better health and quality of life for all our people—will depend in large part on knowledge and technological developments which can come only from scientific research. Science is a critical factor in determining our ability and readiness to meet the problems of the unforeseeable future.[3]

From the outset, the Reagan administration acknowledged that the federal government must provide much of the funding for basic

3. Ibid.

research. Thus, the first statement regarding R & D published by the Reagan Office of Management and Budget (April 1982) stated:

One area of traditional federal responsibility that has been protected from severe reductions in the revised 1982 budget is support of basic research. The Federal government [funds] about 70 percent of all basic research performed in the U.S. Many believe that this investment can be utilized most efficiently if it is accompanied by a measure of long-term stability in funding because basic research is a cumulative process, e.g., gaps created in a period of reduced support cannot be quickly overcome by even a sharp increase in basic research spending at a later date.[4]

The chairman of President Reagan's Council of Economic Advisers told the AAAS annual R & D policy colloquium in June 1981:

Economists are well aware that even in the most supportive environment most areas of basic research still require public support. From my professional perspective this is because basic research is so risky, and because the discoveries it may make are not easily converted to rewards for individual entrepreneurs.[5]

Although the Reagan administration's revisions of the Carter administration's fiscal 1981 and 1982 R & D budgets did result in a real decline in federal funds for basic research, the fiscal 1983 budget provided for real growth of support in basic research of almost 3 percent (depending ultimately on the nation's inflation rate for 1982 and 1983).

Thus, Reagan administration officials have reaffirmed the basic case for public support of science first set down by Vannevar Bush in his seminal 1945 report to President Franklin D. Roosevelt entitled *Science: The Endless Frontier.* Positing a wholly new role for the federal government, Bush stated:

The Government should accept new responsibilities for promoting the flow of new scientific knowledge and the development of scientific talent in our youth. These responsibilities are the proper concern of the Government, for they vitally affect our health, our jobs and our national security. It is in keeping also with basic United States policy that Gov-

4. Office of Management and Budget, "Revised Special Analysis of the R & D Component of the 1981 and 1982 Budgets of the U.S. Government," mimeographed (Washington, D.C., April 1981), p. 2.

5. Albert H. Teich et al., eds., *R & D and the New National Agenda: Federal R & D: Issues in Defense R & D: Agency Perspectives: R & D in the FY 1982 Budget: Impacts* (Washington, D.C.: American Association for the Advancement of Science, 1981), p. 23.

ernment should foster the opening of new frontiers and this is the modern way to do it. For many years the Government has wisely supported research in the agricultural colleges and the benefits have been great. The time has come when such support should be extended to other fields.[6]

The purpose of this monograph is to describe and analyze change and continuity in the intellectual foundation and actual operation of the federal science support system under Presidents Gerald Ford, Jimmy Carter, and Ronald Reagan—with particular emphasis on the Carter and Reagan administrations. The study is confined to the executive branch and does not deal in any detail with congressional responses and initiatives. Nor does it attempt to cover all substantive R & D program areas. Four areas illustrate the general propositions: basic research (across all fields), defense R & D, energy R & D, and space R & D. The study also examines in detail the differences between the Carter and the Reagan administrations in fostering industrial innovation.

Chapter 1 outlines the rationale for federal R & D policy set down by the Ford administration in *Issues '78*, a document that accompanied President Ford's last budget submission to Congress. Chapter 2 analyzes both the underlying precepts of science policy under President Carter and the working out of that policy, as shown by the Carter administration's budget priorities and totals. Chapter 3 presents the policy for science and technology set forth by Reagan administration officials, delineating areas of change and of continuity. Chapter 4 examines the fiscal 1982 and 1983 R & D budgets in light of the policy prescriptions of the Reagan administration. Chapter 5 sets forth tentative policy recommendations that build upon areas of consensus in the last three administrations and attempt to deal with emerging issues and problems in the federal science support system.

6. Vannevar Bush, *Science: The Endless Frontier* (Washington, D.C.: National Science Foundation reprint, 1980), pp. 8–9.

1
The Ford Legacy

President Ford put forward a remarkably thorough rationale for federal R & D policy in his last month in office. It was set down in a document entitled *Issues '78*, which accompanied his last budget submission to Congress.

Issues '78 was only one of several indications of a last flurry of activity within the Ford administration regarding the national R & D effort. In mid-December 1976, President Ford presided over a meeting in the White House of about thirty leading members of the governmental and nongovernmental science establishment, including the heads of the principal federal R & D agencies, several cabinet officers, the presidents of the National Academy of Sciences and National Academy of Engineering, the heads of a number of professional, educational, and public interest organizations, and a number of distinguished university and industry scientists. Led by the director of the newly reestablished White House Office of Science and Technology, H. Guy Stever, the participants reviewed with the president the major decisions underlying the fiscal 1978 R & D budget and the rationale of the administration's science and technology policy.[1]

In January 1977, in his last formal budget message to Congress, the president singled out basic research and defense as the two areas that, even in a time of extreme budgetary pressure, required real increases in the coming year. Ford said that he was proposing an increase in basic research, because "we must maintain our world leadership in science and technology in order to increase our national productivity and attain the better life we want for our people and the rest of the world."[2]

Issues '78, which accompanied the budget message, consisted of a series of papers on various major domestic and defense issues. Prepared by the Office of Management and Budget (OMB) staff, it repre-

1. Willis Shapley et al., *Research and Development in the Federal Budget: FY 1978* (Washington, D.C.: American Association for the Advancement of Science, 1978), p. 9 (hereafter cited as *AAAS Report, 1978*).

2. Office of Management and Budget, *Issues '78: Perspectives on Fiscal Year 1978 Budget* (Washington, D.C., 1977) (hereafter cited as OMB, *Issues '78*).

1

sented not only the views of the outgoing Ford administration but also the ideas of professionals who continue in budget positions through changes of administration. Not surprisingly, therefore, some precepts in *Issues '78* regarding federal R & D policies reappeared in Carter and Reagan administration policy statements.

Overall Rationale. *Issues '78* stated that research and development should be viewed not as an end in itself but as a means of achieving national and agency goals. The federal government invests in R & D to carry out its responsibilities both in such areas as defense and space and in supplying services to the public. In providing services to the public, the federal government also encourages the private and non-profit sectors to invest in R & D both through direct funding and through tax incentives and other indirect means.[3]

The federal government should focus its direct R & D investment in three broad areas:

• direct federal needs, such as defense and space exploration, where the federal government assumes full responsibility for the activity and is the consumer of the product or service

• general economic and human welfare needs, such as basic research, medicine, agriculture, and environmental protection, where major governmental responsibility is accepted because of insufficient incentives for the private sector to invest enough to meet national needs.

• specific national needs, such as new energy technologies and advanced aeronautical research, where the government shares responsibility with the private sector and uses public funds to accelerate and augment private sector activity because of an overriding national interest or a need to supply alternative technological options[4]

In addition to overall budgetary limitations, there are two types of constraints that influence federal R & D decisions:

• the necessity to avoid overtaking private sector responsibilities for producing, marketing, and utilizing technical advances in areas—such as energy conservation in industrial manufacturing—where individual companies are the beneficiaries and have strong financial incentives to complete the technology themselves

• the necessity to avoid government investment in technologies where user demands—and future economic viability—are highly un-

3. Ibid., p. 37.
4. Ibid., p. 38.

certain (the example given by the OMB was high-speed trackless trains)[5]

Basic Research. *Issues '78* devoted a small issue paper to the subject of federal support for basic research. The federal government, it stated, had accepted responsibility for funding basic research in a broad range of disciplines by reason of national interest. National interest was invoked on two grounds: that the general advancement of scientific knowledge is essential to the long-term growth of the national economy and that it is essential to the achievement of national goals in such areas as health, environment, and energy. Thus various federal mission agencies support basic research in order to acquire knowledge for the achievement of their long-range objectives—without regard to specific, short-term practical applications.[6]

Unresolved Issues in Federal R & D Policy. *Issues '78* laid out a series of unresolved issues relating to federal R & D policy, including the following:

Adequacy of total national R & D investment, and the portion of it devoted to basic research. The document took note of the concern of some economists and scientists that the total R & D outlays as a percentage of GNP declined during the late 1960s and the 1970s in the United States, while increasing in other industrial nations. And it expressed agreement with the proposition that there is a link between investment in R & D and innovation and productivity in the civilian industrial sector.

Issues '78 pointed out, however, that "uncertainties and questions continue to exist about whether there is a real problem with respect to the overall level of the U.S. investment in R & D, given the size and diversity of the U.S. effort and given the difficulties in making valid comparisons regarding R & D trends."

The same problems arise in evaluating the state of basic research. The document stated: "Determining the appropriate level of federal support of basic research presents especially difficult conceptual and practical problems because it is impossible to predict in advance where the growth in funding basic research is most likely to contribute to future breakthroughs in fundamental knowledge." Such a determination, therefore, must be based on an "appraisal of the general 'health' of U.S. science."[7]

5. Ibid.
6. Ibid., pp. 41–45.
7. Ibid., p. 39.

3

The Ford administration acknowledged that the decline in real dollars since the late 1960s in the total R & D investment and the decline of about 20 percent for basic research was a cause for concern. The fiscal 1977 and fiscal 1978 budgets reversed the pattern. (In real terms, total R & D outlays increased by 2 percent and basic research by 3 percent between fiscal 1977 and fiscal 1978.)[8]

Government versus private activity. The uncertainties and difficulties of defining appropriate public and private sector roles related largely to the development, demonstration, and commercialization of R & D. The Ford administration acknowledged that it was difficult to decide under what conditions government intervention was appropriate, given general private sector responsibilities for marketing new commercial products and services based on new technologies.

Other federal R & D options. Here the issues revolved around an appropriate mixture of direct and indirect government R & D investment options. These options would include tax incentives and changes in patent policy, antitrust law, and regulatory policy, as well as direct federal procurement and support for civilian industrial R & D.[9]

Priority Program Areas. In discussion papers dealing with high-priority program areas, *Issues '78* fleshed out principles set forth in the overall rationale for federal R & D policy. The separate analyses included energy, space, and defense and the work of the National Science Foundation.

Energy. Energy R & D received the most extensive and exhaustive treatment.[10] The Ford administration coincided with the years immediately following the 1973–1974 oil embargo. Congress had responded to public pressure by continually pressing the administration to "do something" about the energy crisis. In Congress, doing something translated into a strong belief that new and advanced technology offered a way out of the crisis and of a concomitant propensity to pour more resources into energy programs, particularly energy R & D programs.

Members of the Ford administration, particularly the OMB staff, were not entirely in disagreement with congressional sentiments, but they took the opportunity in these *Issues '78* documents to put the energy problems in some perspective. *Issues '78* acknowledged at the

8. Ibid., p. 43.
9. Ibid., p. 39.
10. Ibid., pp. 48–56. See also *AAAS Report, 1978*, pp. 19–20, 49–59.

outset of the energy R & D section that new technologies would over time open new options for energy conservation and production. It cautioned, however, against the idea that technological fixes should be either the first or the most important responses to the U.S. energy predicament. Both energy price deregulation and the institution of reasonable and stable environmental standards were cited as more important governmental actions.

The federal role in energy R & D, stated the document, should be concentrated on those areas where private industry finds it difficult to operate: basic research, where the results are not "capturable";[11] high-risk and high-cost demonstration programs, especially where there are long-term uncertainties about prices of competing energy products; and research to back up energy and environmental regulatory standards.

Federal support was considered less appropriate in areas where "the technical risk is low, development time is relatively short, or an intimate knowledge of the market is required." The federal government was particularly ill equipped to make the necessary decisions for bringing technologies to the marketplace. Thus activities such as marketing, promotion, and technical assistance for products and services should be left to the private sector. Where the federal government did support demonstration programs, a high degree of cost sharing should be required so that private industry would have the necessary stake and incentive to put forward its best managerial and technical resources. "Unlike new defense technologies," noted *Issues '78,* "where cost could be subordinated to other requirements, new energy technologies must be competitive or they will not be manufactured and sold in the marketplace."

The Ford administration gave coal and uranium technologies top priority among the various energy R & D options over the next several decades as substitutes for high-priced oil and gas. It also noted, however, that energy conservation and solar programs might in the long run reduce imported oil and gas dependence.

Coal and uranium shared the following positive traits: they are cheap and abundant; the technologies for producing energy from them are relatively inexpensive and can be rendered reliable, safe, and environmentally acceptable; and the technologies are familiar to utilities and other users. Coal can also be converted into gas or liquid to replace natural gas or oil. Nuclear power, as a complement to coal,

---

11. That is, it is hard for corporations to exercise property rights over the results or products of basic research, and therefore the market does not provide incentives to elicit adequate basic research support.

offers economic and environmental advantages over coal in many regions of the country.

With regard to fossil energy, the Ford fiscal 1978 budget proposed new efforts in coal liquefaction and gasification R & D, as well as major cost-sharing activities in recovering oil from oil shale. The Ford administration, in acknowledging an important government role in *accelerating* the development and demonstration of fossil fuel technologies, noted that large-scale demonstration projects "should be few in number and be separately proposed and approved by the Congress." Thus it continued to hold that the private sector had primary responsibility for the development and commercialization of R & D.

Regarding nuclear energy, sizable increases were proposed for fusion research, for the liquid metal fast breeder reactor program (including construction of the Clinch River breeder reactor demonstration plant), for the fuel cycle and nuclear safeguards program, and for uranium enrichment R & D, especially gas centrifuge enrichment technology.

With regard to energy conservation and solar energy technologies, the Ford administration used *Issues '78* to present its side of a continuing debate with Congress over the proper role of the federal government. Increased federal support should go, the document said, to more long-term basic and applied research activities in these areas, in contrast to "the undue current emphasis" on early demonstrations of technologies that either would not be competitive or did not have the potential to become major contributors to conservation in the near term (for example, electric vehicles). There were also energy conservation technologies and processes that private industry could pick up or that were not in widespread use because of economic or institutional, rather than technological, barriers. Listed as examples for reduced or no federal support were advanced recovery techniques for oil and gas and conservation R & D for buildings and industrial processes. Increases were proposed for the development and demonstration of solar cooling applications rather than hot water or heating, which industry could pick up. For solar electric technologies, the Ford administration proposed research for long-term technological or economic breakthroughs (such as novel materials and devices for photovoltaics) rather than the demonstration of large-scale hardware (again for photovoltaics) that Congress preferred.

In his final budget message to Congress, President Ford endorsed the idea of a Department of Energy. It would consist of the major energy R & D programs in the Energy Research and Development Administration, a number of regulatory and R & D programs from the Federal Energy Administration, and a miscellany of regulatory and R & D programs from the Federal Power Commission, the Department of Interior, and other agencies.[12]

President Ford also supported the establishment of an Energy Independence Authority, with $100 billion in equity and authority to assist in the development and commercialization of emerging new energy technologies.[13] The Energy Independence Authority had been championed by Vice President Nelson Rockefeller. Others in the administration, led by OMB Director James T. Lynn and Council of Economic Advisers Chairman Alan Greenspan, had pointed out that the rationale behind such an entity ran counter to the Ford administration's principles regarding the role of the federal government in energy resource development. Occupying only a brief paragraph in *Issues '78*, the presidential endorsement of the Energy Independence Authority remains evidence of major unresolved differences in Ford administration policy.

Space policy. The central feature of space policy throughout the Ford years was the top priority given to the development of the space shuttle.[14] In fiscal 1978, funding for shuttle development took about 45 percent of the National Aeronautics and Space Administration (NASA) budget. *Issues '78* affirmed the intention of the administration to maintain a "relatively level total dollar investment in the civilian space program" (adjusted annually for inflation). At the fiscal 1978 total budget level ($4 billion), this allowed for the continuation of a balanced but constricted space program in which all of the major elements of the space budget—shuttle, space science, space applications, and aeronautical research—could be supported.

The fiscal 1978 space budget continued several important programs, such as the launch of the High Energy Astronomy Observatory; the launch in 1977 of two Mariner spacecraft to explore Jupiter and Saturn; the launch in 1978 of the third earth resources technology satellite, LANDSAT-C; and a joint government–private sector research program to reduce aircraft fuel consumption. It also added new initiatives, including a space telescope ($450 million over seven years), a Jupiter orbiter probe mission ($280 million over five years), and a fourth advanced-technology satellite to survey earth resources (LANDSAT-D, $180 million over six years).

Probably at the urging of the OMB professional staff, *Issues '78* attempted to head off early initiation of an expensive space project: the manned earth-orbiting space station. Funding for design and

12. OMB, *Issues '78*, pp. 92–99.
13. Ibid., p. 86.
14. OMB, *Issues '78*, pp. 57–62. See also *AAAS Report, 1978*, pp. 59–61.

engineering studies for the project was deferred. Explaining this deferral, *Issues '78* warned that before a decision was made, there would have to be a full-scale review of U.S. space and aeronautics goals; there would have to be a demonstrated absolute value of such a space station against existing capabilities (such as the space shuttle); overall federal budget constraints might require other high-priority space projects to be scrapped if this station went forward; and in any case, total costs of such a station were highly conjectural, ranging from $1 billion to $5 billion.

Defense R & D. Defense spending became the focus of debate during the 1976 presidential campaign. Concluding that defense spending had been inadequate and reacting to criticisms from Ronald Reagan and others in the Republican party, President Ford proposed real increases in defense spending of 6 percent and 8 percent for fiscal years 1978 and 1979. Candidate Jimmy Carter, in contrast, campaigned on a pledge to cut defense by $5 billion to $7 billion.[15]

Malcolm R. Currie, director of defense research and engineering under President Ford, left a 350-page valedictory statement regarding national defense R & D priorities. The statement argued strongly for stepped-up activity in a number of areas to "reverse some dangerously developing trends in the balance of military technology." "The United States," said Currie in a sentence that stated the major theme of the treatise, "must maintain a position of unequivocal technological superiority." Currie called for a sustained real annual growth in defense R & D of between 6 percent and 10 percent.[16]

Issues '78 identified R & D as the key element in the Ford administration's drive to achieve an "accelerated modernization of both strategic and general purpose forces." To this end, Ford's fiscal 1978 budget proposed an increase of 12.1 percent in defense R & D over the fiscal 1977 figure, to $12 billion from $10.6 billion.

With regard to strategic forces, the Ford budget called for completion of the B-1 bomber, continuation of the Trident II submarine design studies, Minuteman missile improvements, MX mobile ICBM engineering development, and the development of air, surface, and submarine cruise missiles.

For the general-purpose forces, the areas of concentration were improved communications for land and sea warfare, a family of air defense weapons against saturation air attack, increased mobility and firepower for land forces, ship defenses against cruise missiles, mod-

15. OMB, *Issues '78*, pp. 7–24. See also *AAAS Report, 1978*, pp. 44–48.
16. *AAAS Report, 1978*, pp. 46–47.

ernization of avionics and air-to-air missile systems, and, finally, development of an advanced attack helicopter.

In his departing statement, Currie particularly singled out as a top priority strengthening the "technology base" of defense R & D (R & D associated with the technology base includes a number of activities under the budget categories of research, exploratory development, and advanced development, a total of about $2 billion in the fiscal 1978 defense R & D budget). Currie also stressed the need to continue rebuilding the Department of Defense relationship with universities. He recommended greater financial outlays and support of wider-ranging projects than had been possible when the restrictive Mansfield Amendment held sway.[17]

National Science Foundation. Issues '78 took special note of the place of the National Science Foundation (NSF) in the accomplishment of federal science policy.[18] The establishment of the NSF in 1950 marked the symbolic acceptance by the federal government of its primary "responsibility for supporting basic research in the broad national interest, recognizing that the private sector does not invest adequately, and that basic research funding by the various federal mission agencies in support of their own program objectives would not be sufficient to serve the overall national need." The Ford administration also argued that the NSF had a role in funding applied research (specifically through the Research Applied to National Needs program, which supported programs that fall between or transcend the responsibilities of individual federal mission agencies) and a role in the improvement of science education.

For fiscal 1978, the total NSF budget went up 13 percent, support for research in the scientific disciplines (such as biology, mathematics, and chemistry) rising 12 percent and applied research 22 percent, largely as a result of a substantial increase in an initiative for earthquake hazard reduction. *Issues '78* also noted the need to apply federal dollars to upgrade and replace scientific equipment at colleges and universities. Science education activities received $76 million in fiscal 1978 in support of programs to develop new material for science teaching, equipment for school laboratories, and programs to attract more women and minorities into scientific careers.

17. Ibid., p. 48. The Mansfield Amendment was an amendment to the Military Authorization Act of 1970 (Public Law 90-121 Section 203) that restricted the use of defense R & D funds to projects having a "direct or apparent relationship to a specific military function or operation." Although the language was loosened somewhat a year later, the amendment continued for some years to have a negative impact on Defense Department support of broad-gauged basic research.

18. OMB, *Issues '78*, pp. 45–47.

2

Science and Technology Policy under President Carter

From 1977 to 1981, the Carter administration in its statements and actions regarding science and technology policy continued along lines laid down by the Ford administration, but also introduced new directions of its own. Much of the rationale for federal government support of science and technology remained the same, though the Carter White House placed its own nuances and emphases on this rationale. In energy and other specific program areas, it instituted major policy and priority changes. In defense and some other areas, the Carter administration's own rationale and actions changed substantially in the course of the four years.

The Carter administration used a variety of forums to present its views and policies on science and technology. There were two special messages to Congress, one directly on science and technology policy, the other on industrial innovation. Carter singled out R & D for special attention on several occasions in budget messages and State of the Union addresses. Beginning in 1978, there were annual science and technology reports to Congress, as prescribed by the National Science and Technology Policy, Organization and Priorities Act of 1976. Top Carter administration officials, particularly the science adviser, Frank Press, appeared occasionally before congressional committees. Finally, the annual R & D policy colloquia of the American Association for the Advancement of Science increasingly contained comprehensive and searching exchanges between national policy makers and scientists regarding the current status and future directions of federal science and technology policy.[1]

1. Public Papers of the Presidents, *Jimmy Carter (1979)*, "Science and Technology, Message to Congress, March 27, 1979," pp. 528–46; idem, "Industrial Innovation Initiatives, Message to Congress, October 31, 1979," pp. 2070–74; National Science Foundation, *Science and Technology: Annual Report to Congress (1979)* and *Science and Technology: Annual Report to Congress (1980)*; Don I. Phillips et al., eds., *Research and Development in the Federal Budget: Colloquium Proceedings, June 15–16, 1977* (Washington, D.C.: AAAS, 1977) (hereafter cited as *AAAS Colloquium, 1977*); Don I. Phillips et al.,

Overall Rationale

In explaining the public benefits of support for science and technology programs, officials of the Carter administration emphasized two themes: the importance of science and technology in solving the nation's major domestic and national security problems and the significance of scientific and technological advances in increasing productivity and economic growth.

Thus President Carter stated in his March 1979 special message to Congress on science and technology: "While science and technology alone will not solve all our domestic problems they hold the key to many aspects of the solutions. . . . We expect science and technology to find new sources of energy, to feed the world's growing population, to provide new tools for our national security."[2] Much of the content of the special message constituted a detailed delineation of the contributions of science and technology to the solutions of problems in particular program areas such as energy, the environment, health, natural resource development, agricultural production, and national security.

At the outset of the Carter administration, William Nordhaus, a member of the president's Council of Economic Advisers, linked scientific and technological advance to economic growth. At the American Association for the Advancement of Science R & D policy colloquium in June 1977, Nordhaus stated:

> Science and research are both central to the long-term growth in living standards—without question technological advance is a key input into the process of achieving increased productivity. Technological advance enables us to use resources more efficiently; to get more output from the same BTUs; to find new uses for existing resources; to find uses for previously "useless" materials and concepts; to create new types of goods and to improve old ones. In short, whether in defense or civilian life, new technologies enable society to get "more bang for the buck."[3]

---

eds., *R & D in the Federal Budget: R & D, Industry and the Economy: Colloquium Proceedings, June 20–21, 1978* (Washington, D.C.: AAAS, 1978) (hereafter cited as *AAAS Colloquium, 1978*); Don I. Phillips et al., eds., *Federal R & D: R & D, Industry and the Economy; International Aspects of R & D; Colloquium Proceedings, June 19–20, 1979* (Washington, D.C.: AAAS, 1979) (hereafter cited as *AAAS Colloquium, 1979*); Albert H. Teich et al., eds., *R & D in an Inflationary Environment: Federal R & D, Industry and the Economy; Universities; and Intergovernmental Science; Colloquium Proceedings, June 19–20, 1980* (hereafter cited as *AAAS Colloquium, 1980*).

2. Public Papers, *Carter,* pp. 528, 531.

3. *AAAS Colloquium, 1977,* pp. 20–21, 32.

The Carter administration also added a significant nuance, at least symbolically, to the rationale for a federal role in support of R & D. In a number of policy statements, federal R & D dollars were presented as an investment rather than merely an annual budget expense. Thus Carter said in his 1979 State of the Union message:

> Scientific research and development is an investment in the nation's future, essential for all fields, from health, agriculture, and environment to energy, space, and defense. We are enhancing the search for the causes of disease; we are undertaking research to anticipate and prevent significant environmental hazards; we are increasing research in astronomy; we will maintain our leadership in space science; and we are pushing back the frontiers in basic research for energy, defense, and other critical national needs.[4]

Too much should not be made of this rhetorical shift—R & D programs, though somewhat protected, felt the budgetary pinch during the last two Carter budgets—but it does signify an important revision and advance in the attitude of government officials toward public expenditures for science and technology, particularly basic research.

The Carter administration retained the OMB professional staff's general definitions and explanations of the role of federal support of R & D and the focus of federal dollars. Thus all the special analyses accompanying the budgets noted three needs that governed federal R & D obligations and outlays: (1) direct federal needs, where the government is the sole or primary user (defense, space, air traffic control); (2) general economic and social needs, where government assumes responsibility because there is insufficient incentive for the private sector to invest adequately (basic research and some health and agricultural research); (3) specific national needs, where the government seeks to accelerate and augment private sector R & D efforts because of overriding national interest or because of the need to increase the number of technological options.[5]

During the course of the Carter administration, the broadly defined area of "specific national needs" provided the basis for stepped-up government activity further along the "D" part of the R & D spectrum. This was particularly true in energy, where Carter administration officials moved toward a closer collaboration between the government and private enterprise. Thus in a 1980 address to the AAAS R & D policy colloquium, Energy Department Deputy Secre-

4. Public Papers, *Carter*, p. 140.

5. Office of Management and Budget, *Special Analyses: Budget of the United States Government, Fiscal Year 1979*, p. 305 (hereafter cited as *OMB Special Analysis, 1979*).

tary John C. Sawhill affirmed the Carter administration's goal of creating a synthetic fuels industry that produced the equivalent of 2 million barrels of oil per day:

> An industry capable of capturing the potential of these resources will not happen by itself, certainly not in the time frame we believe necessary. So the federal government is taking a leadership role to research and develop broad-based technologies, to assess environmental and social impacts, to provide financial incentives, and to remove unnecessary regulatory obstacles.[6]

In energy, transportation, and the promotion of industrial innovation in general, the positing of an urgent national need was used to justify federal support to accelerate the rate of development of new technologies. The tendency of the Carter administration to inject the federal government more and more into demonstration and commercialization activities in areas it considered of high national priority would contrast greatly with the more rigorously applied free-market theories of the Reagan administration.

Basic Research. The Carter administration from the outset adopted the view, which originated during the last two years of the Ford administration, that the substantial decline in federal support for basic research since the late 1960s, if allowed to continue, would have grave consequences for the United States. In one of the first detailed statements by a Carter OMB political official, in 1977, W. Bowman Cutter, executive associate director of the OMB, told the annual American Association for the Advancement of Science R & D policy colloquium that "there is ample reason to be concerned about the trends" and the consequences stemming from the fact that "federal investment in basic research declined by 20 percent in real terms from 1967 to 1975."

Cutter went on to outline the case for a predominant role for the federal government in the support of basic research:

> Let me start with . . . conclusions which represent, I think, where OMB institutionally has come out [with regards to basic research]. First, the federal government has a responsibility to fund basic research and R & D both to solve national problems and to permit sustained economic growth. . . .
>
> Basic research is undeniably a public issue. First . . . there is strong evidence about the positive role of knowledge and knowledge increases in economic growth. . . . Second, one can presume, it's a presumption I make in any case, that the

---

6. *AAAS Colloquium, 1980,* p. 62.

knowledge base depends on basic research and R & D and, at least in a reasonably direct sense, on our investment in them. Third, there is considerable plausibility to the argument that the private sector will not invest sufficiently in basic research. . . . There are two reasons for this:

1. First, it is very difficult for private firms . . . to be confident about appropriating the gains of successful basic research. . . .

2. The second point is uncertainty . . . the uncertainty of when those gains will accrue, the uncertainty of where they will accrue, and the uncertainty of in what areas of research they will accrue. . . . And finally, one concludes from these statements that the public sector or the federal government must invest, if the social investment in basic research . . . is to be sufficient.[7]

President Carter personally took the lead in attempting to persuade Congress that full support for basic research was in the national interest. During the congressional budget deliberations in 1978, Carter wrote to the chairmen of all committees and subcommittees responsible for basic research funding to persuade them to protect basic research appropriations:

I want to emphasize that even relatively small reductions in key agencies—such as the National Science Foundation—or in new initiatives and growth planned for the mission agencies—including NASA and the Departments of Agriculture, Energy and Defense—would defeat our objective. Modest increases in real growth in these programs are necessary if we are to strengthen the nation's capacity and productivity in critical areas of research.[8]

In his review of the science and technology accomplishments of the Carter administration, Carter's science adviser, Press, in an interview with *Science* magazine, placed at the top of his list policies "emphasizing growth in the support of basic research" and noted that of key importance "from the policy viewpoint was the President's decision to view basic research as an investment rather than an expense."[9]

In the same retrospective article, however, Press also mentioned some of the problems associated with federal support of basic research. There are, he wrote, "no established criteria and procedures

7. *AAAS Colloquium, 1977*, pp. 13–15.

8. Quoted in address by Frank Press, *AAAS Colloquium, 1978*, p. 18.

9. Frank Press, "Science and Technology in the White House, 1977 to 1980: Part I," *Science*, January 9, 1981, p. 140.

for determining the adequacy of the existing science and technology base or for identifying an adequate level of support for research, particularly basic research." He went on:

> Relevant factors include levels of activity in various scientific fields and the anticipated benefits or costs of incremental changes in level of support; the potential opportunity costs of not funding given areas of research; the effects of past concentration of support on research capabilities, institutions and facilities; the opportunities available to young scientists; the views of employers on the quantity and quality of new scientists and engineers; and the policies of other countries. . . . Ultimately, however, policymakers must decide on appropriate levels of research on the basis of imperfect indicators, information from many disparate sources, and many uncertainties.[10]

The lack of direct criteria for judging the adequacy of the total basic research budget and the difficulty of judging between competing basic research areas complicated the task of defending basic research in times of budgetary stringency. Over the course of the Carter administration the seemingly intractable problems of inflation and slow economic growth worked to press the budget screws ever tighter.

The effect of these forces was quite evident in Cutter's remarks to the AAAS R & D policy symposium in the summer of 1980, three years after his first statement to the symposium. In terms that struck chords much like those of the Reagan administration one year later, Cutter painted a sobering though not despairing picture of the pressures on the federal basic science support system. Regarding the economic and budgetary outlook, he stated:

> As we look at receipts, at the applications of current tax law to the economy, and particularly at inflation rates over the next few years and the greater vulnerability of the economy to inflation, we see tax burdens rising to the highest point in American history.
>
> Now, what do these two factors suggest? They suggest that on the current track we will inexorably increase the budget as a percentage of GNP, and at the same time we will see tax burdens rising. They further suggest that there will be both policy reactions and, in a sense, national political reactions against both developments. I do not think that the trends are automatic. . . . I suspect that there will be tax cuts over the next several years which will solve to a degree the tax burden

10. Ibid., p. 141.

problem but will exacerbate the budget problem and exacerbate our inflation problems. . . . [This] will impose even greater pressures on the budget than we have seen in the past few years. . . . Finally, because such a high proportion of the budget is uncontrollable in a constrained budget time I see the discretionary programs being eroded year by year, inexorably—again, unless we do something about it. To put in a bottom line, I see an exceedingly constrained budget picture over the next several years, with the uncontrollables growing as a percentage of the budget, and consequently, the discretionary programs in the budget coming under constant and severe pressure.[11]

Cutter then went on to note the implications for basic research, which, he said, was an "absolutely critical" long-run investment but which would suffer in the short run. To offset the pressures, he stated:

We are going to have to look with increasing rigor at R & D and basic research. If we are going to carry out our task, which I believe fundamentally is to protect basic research and keep it growing in sensible ways, then we are also going to have to look to increasing rigor of analysis—an increasing emphasis on relating the basic research and the R & D that we do to sectors and areas that are truly important to us, and to clearly understanding the nature of the other claims on the budget. . . . [The question will be] are we spending our money on basic research in areas where, at least in our perception, the nation has clear needs in the long run? . . . I do not believe that [these judgments] should involve a requirement that one stipulate in advance the outputs from basic research; I do not think one can do that. But they do require rigor from us as to the role of the federal government in specific investments.[12]

Carter basic research budgets. Against increasing pressures, the Carter administration achieved its purpose of protecting basic research. Between the first Carter budget in fiscal 1978 and the last one in January 1981 (fiscal 1982 budget), the federal basic research budget rose from $3.3 billion to $5.9 billion. According to the calculations of the AAAS, this translated to real growth (in constant 1972 dollars) of $2.2 billion to $2.5 billion, or about 14 percent over the five-year period.[13]

11. *AAAS Colloquium, 1980*, p. 41.

12. Ibid., p. 42.

13. These numbers were taken from compilations made by the American Association for the Advancement of Science throughout the period: see, for instance, *AAAS Report*,

Within this period, between fiscal 1978 and 1980, funds for basic research (in constant 1972 dollars) rose from $2.2 billion to $2.4 billion, then remained level at $2.4 billion in fiscal 1980 and 1981, and finally rose again to $2.5 billion in fiscal 1982.[14]

Between fiscal 1978 and fiscal 1982, the major change in basic research priorities among agencies was the rise in the place of defense, from fifth to third. In fiscal 1978, agency totals in descending order were Health, Education, and Welfare (HEW) (largely National Institutes of Health (NIH)) $793 million, National Science Foundation (NSF) $688 million, Energy Research and Development Administration (ERDA) $427 million, National Aeronautics and Space Administration (NASA) $365 million, and Defense $324 million. In fiscal 1982, the revised standings were HEW (largely NIH) $2,045 million, NSF $1,063 million, Defense $714 million, Energy $710 million, and NASA $681 million.[15]

Demonstration, Development, Commercialization. When one moves beyond basic research toward the demonstration and development end of the R & D spectrum, the rationale for public support becomes confused and the decisions more difficult to make. The Carter administration, like the preceding Ford and succeeding Reagan administrations, struggled with mixed success to resolve the difficulties.

In his special message to Congress on science and technology in March 1979, President Carter stated that there was a case for the expenditure of public resources beyond basic research "where there is a national need to accelerate the development of new technologies in the private sector." He went on:

> This is especially true when the risk is great or the costs inordinately high, such as with many aspects of energy and transportation. However, we look to private industry to finance research and development activities having near-term commercial payoff. Industry is most sensitive to the marketplace, to the benefits of competition and to commercialization of new technologies.[16]

As propounded by the president, the ground rules for federal intervention at the demonstration and development stages seemed

1979, p. 15; *AAAS Report, 1980*, p. 23; *AAAS Report, 1981*, pp. 16–17; *AAAS Report, 1982*, pp. 5–6.

14. Ibid.

15. These numbers were compiled by the AAAS; comparable numbers compiled by the NSF would differ somewhat, but the agency rankings would remain the same. *AAAS Report, 1978*, p. 32; and *AAAS Report, 1982*, p. 23.

16. Public Papers, *Carter,* pp. 529–30.

relatively simple and straightforward; in practice, they often were stretched and breached. Divisions began within the administration over what constituted areas of overriding national need, when costs were likely to be inordinate for the private sector, and when the public payoffs would be high. The administration's divided mind was magnified in Congress; and special interest groups, always ready to push individual pet projects, were constantly pressuring for new or increased funding for demonstration and development programs.

Bowman Cutter, executive associate director of the OMB, in his first appearance before the annual AAAS R & D symposium, signaled the perplexities and crosscurrents regarding the government role in development and commercialization:

> A problem that we faced throughout last year's budget and that we will face in this year's budget and clearly in coming years' budgets is what should the federal government support beyond basic research. The economic argument for investment in basic research is clear and unassailable. . . . [But] the further one gets towards classical, commercial development, the more problems . . . OMB has institutionally . . . with federal expenditures. There is clearly a grey area in which we begin to leave federal and public expenditure investments, which we are quite certain yield a public return, and we begin to enter into investment about which we have many more doubts.[17]

The OMB, in the special analyses that accompanied annual budgets, continually weighed in with cautions regarding the need to avoid overtaking activities that are more appropriately those of the private sector, such as development; producing and marketing new products and processes (OMB cited solar heating technology as an example); the need to avoid investing in technology where user demand or future economic viability and institutional acceptance are highly unlikely (OMB cited the breeder reactor as an example); and the need to avoid overinvesting in multiple demonstrations of somewhat similar technologies that promise only marginal improvements (OMB cited coal gasification demonstration projects as an example).[18]

In the summer of 1980, in his last appearance before the AAAS R & D symposium, Cutter, looking back over his own experience in the last three years and taking note of the far greater pressures on R & D funds from the administration's attempts to curb inflation and

17. *AAAS Colloquium, 1978*, p. 26.

18. *OMB Special Analysis, 1979*, p. 305; Office of Management and Budget, *Special Analyses: Budget of the United States Government, Fiscal Year 1981*, p. 303 (hereafter cited as *OMB Special Analysis, 1981*).

hold down the overall federal budget, expressed even greater concern about the federal expenditures for demonstration and development activities:

> There is very clear evidence that on the far end of the spectrum . . . we do in fact replace the private sector if we are not careful. I have seen it happen, I have had private coalitions come to me and argue that they needed a particular kind of demonstration plant . . . a particular kind of commercialization project—not because they could not fund it, but because some other group had received funds by the federal government; therefore, it was competitively disadvantageous for them to do it out of their own equity. The less we are cautious about that, the more we will wind up with the federal government simply replacing private investment and private innovation.[19]

Cutter predicted that in the future the administration and the OMB would define the federal role in the R & D spectrum "more and more explicit . . . to make absolutely certain that the investments that we do carry out are those that are appropriate, not simply in the sense of whether or not it is proper etiquette for the federal government to do it, but in the sense of whether it is not wasteful of resources."[20]

Specific Program Area Policies and Priorities

What follows is an analysis of policies instituted and followed by the Carter administration in key R & D program areas—energy, space, defense, and the promotion of industrial innovation. In each case, the degree to which general administration principles regarding R & D policy were realized, diluted, or ignored will be illustrated.

Energy. Two factors exercised the most important influences over the energy R & D budgets of the Carter administration. The first was a revised energy policy strategy that gave energy conservation, renewable energy resources (solar, wind), and fossil fuel development top priority for the short and medium term. It also downgraded nuclear power and opposed development of the breeder reactor. Thus in his 1979 message to Congress on science, President Carter said:

> My near-term program . . . emphasizes conservation, the reduced consumption of oil where alternatives are available.

19. *AAAS Colloquium, 1980,* p. 43.
20. Ibid., p. 42.

This country is blessed with a uniquely abundant supply of energy in the form of coal and oil shale. Over one-third of the known world reserves for coal belong to the United States. A major challenge is to demonstrate technologies that will enable us to substitute these energy sources for our ever increasing oil imports.[21]

The second factor was the continuing ambivalence and indecision about the proper role of the federal government in the demonstration, development, and commercialization of energy technologies.

Priorities. The final budget submitted by President Ford would have given nuclear programs 64 percent of the total energy R & D budget; the revised fiscal 1978 budget under President Carter reduced that figure to 57 percent. Four years later, when Carter submitted his last budget, nuclear R & D received only 41 percent of the total energy R & D funds.[22] There were also major changes within the nuclear R & D budget. The Carter administration proposed to cancel the Clinch River breeder reactor demonstration plant on two grounds: the demonstration was premature and uneconomic; and liquid metal fast breeder reactors would produce weapons grade plutonium as a byproduct and thus would complicate the administration's efforts to stem the proliferation of nuclear weapons. (The battle over the breeder reactor went on for the four years of the Carter administration, with congressional supporters of the project ultimately winning out.) Nuclear waste management, alternative breeder concepts, and advanced light-water reactor development all received increased emphasis and support in the Carter nuclear R & D budgets.[23]

The proper federal role. The Carter administration's energy R & D policies and programs provide a case study of the difficulties attendant to defining the proper federal role in a program area that is characterized by heavy external pressures and the perception of national crisis, by high congressional interest, and by the desire of special interest groups to tap public funds. The energy section of President Carter's science and technology message to Congress also illustrates the divided mind of the administration on the division of responsibilities between the public and private sectors. In discussing the need to demonstrate and develop new energy technologies, Car-

21. Public Papers, *Carter,* p. 532.

22. *AAAS Report, 1978,* p. 53; *AAAS Report, 1982,* p. 28.

23. *OMB Special Analysis, 1979,* p. 316; *OMB Special Analysis, 1981,* p. 316; Department of Energy, *The National Energy Plan II* (Washington, D.C.: 1979), vol. 1, pp. 14–25; *AAAS Report, 1980,* pp. 38–39; *AAAS Report, 1981,* pp. 31–32.

ter noted that "in working with the private sector, it is important that the government . . . not displace the resources [of private] industry."

At the same time, however, Carter laid out a broad role for the federal government:

> A major challenge is to demonstrate technologies that will enable us to substitute [coal and oil shale energy sources] for our ever increasing oil imports. My program provides for the government to work closely with American industry to accelerate the *demonstration of commercial-scale technologies that show promise of entering feasibility and the economics of conversion processes.* [italics added][24]

This statement thus projected a role for the federal government far along the R & D spectrum into support for the technical feasibility of commercial-size plants and, of more significance, into questions of the economics of new technologies.

The OMB, meanwhile, throughout the Carter administration remained a focal point of a much narrower view of the role of the federal government in supporting energy R & D. In the special analysis that accompanied the fiscal 1979 budget, for instance, the OMB stated that "federal investments in 'civilian' R & D . . . reflect a growing realization that the appropriate role of the government is to emphasize longer-term [relatively lower cost] research for the future and new technology options rather than major commercial scale [and relatively higher cost] demonstrations."[25] The document went on to reiterate OMB's standard warnings regarding the need to avoid overtaking private sector activity, to avoid investing in projects of dubious economic viability, and to avoid multiple demonstrations of similar technologies.

Actual program support. The Carter administration, like the Ford administration, resisted congressional efforts to continue to fund large-scale commercial demonstrations of solar hot-water and solar heating devices for residential and commercial buildings. The Carter administration to the end remained adamant against the Clinch River breeder reactor project, though in reality its opposition stemmed more from nuclear nonproliferation considerations than from deeply held beliefs regarding the proper federal role in support of R & D.

In a number of areas, however, the Carter administration ignored the admonitions of the OMB. Asserting overriding national needs or priorities, it supported activities and programs that placed the federal

24. Public Papers, *Carter,* pp. 532–33.
25. *OMB Special Analysis, 1979,* p. 307.

government far down the R & D demonstration, development, and commercialization spectrum.

There was continual expansion of the federal R & D role, particularly in the areas of renewable energy sources (such as solar, wind, and biomass) and conservation, where there was substantial support from within the administration and from Congress. The special analysis of the fiscal 1981 budget, for instance, noted that the "overall increase of 20 percent in solar applications funding will expand activities necessary to establish cost and performance goals in the marketplace and to facilitate market development."[26] Although it drastically reduced the federal role in solar heating technology, the Carter administration planned a major effort to prove the technical feasibility and the commercial and economic viability of solar photovoltaics technology. The administration explained the challenge of photovoltaics and its goals for the programs:

> Many promising forms of renewable resource utilization are not commercial at present, even with the support of credits. . . . For example, photovoltaic cells, which produce electricity directly from sunlight, have declined in cost by more than three orders of magnitude over the past decade, due almost entirely to Government investment. They remain uncompetitive, except for a few specialized applications. Government spending on photovoltaics is now focused on reducing the costs of installed photovoltaic systems to the point of commercial viability.[27]

It also supported similar programs to prove technical feasibility and economic performance in ocean thermal energy, wind energy, and agricultural energy.

The secretary of transportation in 1978 proclaimed that, in conjunction with private industry, the government intended to "reinvent" the automobile. To this end, the Carter administration underwrote programs to produce advanced automobile engines and to perfect electric and hybrid vehicles.[28]

The energy conservation division of the Department of Energy supported a large number of projects to introduce new means of conserving energy in industrial processes and building construction

26. *OMB Special Analysis, 1981*, p. 316.

27. Ibid., p. 398; see also Department of Energy, *National Energy Plan II*, vol. 6, pp. 10–12.

28. National Science Foundation, *The Five-Year Outlook*, vol. 1 (Washington, D.C., 1980), pp. 56–57, and *The Five-Year Outlook*, vol. 2 (Washington, D.C., 1980), pp. 440–41; *OMB Special Analysis, 1981*, pp. 390–91; Department of Energy, *National Energy Plan II*, vol. 3, pp. 11–15.

and maintenance. In recounting its successes in a 1981 document, the department's Industrial Energy Conservation Office listed the following examples: a coil-coating process to reduce the use of natural gas in manufacturing sheet metal and heavy appliances, the development of a grain-drying furnace fueled by cornstalks, the development of an efficient slot-forge furnace for preparing steel for forging, the development of high-temperature recuperators to recapture and reuse waste heat, and the demonstration of efficient fuel-flexible cogeneration systems.[29] A case can be made for the energy conservation payoffs of these programs. Most of them, however, would not pass the Carter administration's test of constituting high-risk or costly technologies or new processes that private industry could not or would not itself underwrite if energy prices and market conditions were right.

Synthetic fuels. More than any other program area, synthetic fuels pointed up the contradictions between the rationale for federal withdrawal from demonstration, development, and commercialization and the realities of political pressures, resulting from the sense of urgency to do something about the energy crisis. The Carter administration initially voiced considerable skepticism concerning the rapid development of a synthetic fuels industry: influential environmentalists within the administration, who stressed conservation, joined forces with OMB skeptics, who doubted the ability of the government to hasten technological progress. Suddenly in the summer of 1979, however, in an attempt to bolster his weakening political fortunes, President Carter announced his support of a massive effort to create a commercially viable synthetic fuels industry by 1990. Carter's espousal of a synthetic fuels commercialization program resulted in the passage by Congress in June 1980 of the Energy Security Act, which created, among other things, a Synthetic Fuels Corporation and committed $88 billion of federal funds over ten years to synthetic fuels development. The Synthetic Fuels Corporation, the Carter administration stated, was "designed to accomplish a single purpose—the acceleration of synthetic fuels commercialization, particularly coal-based synthetics, oil shale and biomass." The corporation was given wide latitude to use price guarantees, purchase agreements, loan guarantees, direct loans, and joint ventures to achieve its purposes.[30]

29. Office of Industrial Programs, Deprtment of Energy, "Summary of Key Accomplishments," internal staff memorandum, March 1981.

30. *OMB Special Analysis, 1981*, p. 393. For an excellent analysis of the legislative history of the Energy Security Corporation and the creation of the Energy Security Fund—as well as a review of the federal government's activities in this area up to

The decision to inject the federal government so deeply into synthetic fuels development and commercialization raised fundamental questions about federal intervention in the R & D spectrum. Of the three OMB cautions regarding federal investments in civilian R & D, the first (the danger of overtaking the private sector) was violated outright: the Synthetic Fuels Corporation, by the basic terms of the power and authority given it, will be making judgments regarding technological promise and economic viability that are traditionally left to private companies. The second caution (low probability of economic viability) may also loom large in later years because of the highly uncertain price of the products of the new processes and of the environmental consequences (not the least of which are the enormous demands on the water supply in the West that many synthetic fuel technologies entail). As for the third OMB caution (avoiding overinvestment in similar technologies and technologies that promise only marginal improvements), the history of industry response to the lure of billions of dollars of federal largesse makes it seem quite real. At the end of 1981, the Synthetic Fuels Corporation had before it over sixty proposals, including almost twenty for closely related coal gasification projects, over fifteen for coal liquefaction projects, fourteen for shale oil, six for tar sands, and five for heavy oil extraction.[31]

Carter administration science and budget officials were hard pressed to defend the massive synthetic fuels programs against accepted ideas about the proper conditions of federal intervention in R & D. In his *Science* magazine retrospective concerning Carter science and technology, presidential science adviser Frank Press ignored the contradiction when discussing synthetic fuels. Press noted that there was a place for the federal government to undertake R & D

> where there is a national need to accelerate the rate of development of new technologies in the private sector. . . . This is especially true when the risk is great, costs inordinately high or time particularly pressing, as with many aspects of alternative energy technologies. In such cases, the government may provide incentives such as direct grants and contracts, guaranteed loans, purchase contracts at guaranteed prices, joint ventures, or, as a last resort, construction of government-owned facilities. Fusion research and development and the recently created Synthetic Fuels Corporation . . . are examples of governmental involvement in an area of national need.

mid-1981—see Carrol E. Watts, "The U.S. Synthetic Fuels Program: An Overview," mimeographed (Washington, D.C.: Government Research Corporation, 1981), passim.

31. Watts, "U.S. Synthetic Fuels Program," pp. 49–59, and app. A.

In the very next paragraph of his article, however, Press said:

We look to the private sector . . . to finance research and development activities having near-term commercial payoff and to bear the major financial responsibility for required capital investment in such cases as synthetic fuels commercialization. Industry is more knowledgeable about the marketplace and sensitive to opportunities for commercialization of new technologies.[32]

Press thus chose to have it both ways and leave it to his readers to decide which route was right.

Commenting on the disparity between rhetoric and practice in the Carter administration's definition of public and private roles in support of R & D, the R & D report of the AAAS stated in 1979:

When new emergencies are recognized, like environmental and energy problems, a major part of the federal response is to step up R & D. So the general government policy that civil sector R & D should be done and paid for by industry and others in the private sector in practice comes down to little more than a presumption in favor of leaving R & D to industry unless the government decides otherwise.[33]

Space. In its larger outlines, the Carter administration's policy toward space and space R & D continued the basic policies of the Ford administration. President Carter took an active interest in the space program and devoted separate sections to it in three of his State of the Union messages (1978, 1979, and 1980). Like President Ford, President Carter gave completion of the space shuttle the highest priority, while committing himself to maintaining a balanced space program. Some priority was given to space application projects, but only base levels of support were given to space science and planetary exploration and to aeronautical research.

In his special message to Congress on science, President Carter stated:

With the advent of the Space Shuttle, we are entering a new era. . . . We will emphasize applications not only by NASA but also by other federal agencies, foreign governments and the private sector. The policy stresses the use of space technologies to meet human needs here on earth. . . . My space policy also encourages continued investigation of the universe. . . .

32. Press, "Science and Technology," pp. 140–41.
33. *AAAS Report, 1979*, p. 66.

It is important that we maintain our world leadership in space. . . . We will provide adequate resources to maintain that leadership.[34]

Through increasingly difficult conditions, the Carter administration did strive to balance completion of the shuttle with continued support and advances in the other areas of space policy—aeronautics, science, and space applications. Two factors operated to constrict the space program: first, overall budgetary restrictions, which bore down ever more tightly during the four years of the Carter administration; and second, the technical difficulties, delays, and concomitant cost overruns that plagued the space shuttle programs throughout the Carter presidency.

By 1981, NASA had spent some $10 billion on the space shuttle project and was expected to spend at least $4 billion more to make the system fully operational (critics of the shuttle charged that it would take an additional $8 billion to make the system operate). On several occasions, from 1977 to 1981, NASA was forced to go back to Congress for supplemental appropriations for the shuttle. The declining costs of shuttle development had been expected to relieve the pressure on other space projects; instead, rising shuttle costs increased budgetary pressure on these programs. The shuttle continued throughout the period to consume more than 50 percent of NASA's budget. As a result, from 1977 to 1981 the space agency was continually forced to postpone the introduction of new projects and stretch out the development time of others.

The total NASA budget authority under President Carter increased from $4.1 billion in fiscal 1978 to a proposed $6.7 billion in the outgoing Carter administration's fiscal 1982 budget. It should be noted, however, that much of this increase came as the Carter administration was leaving office—a whopping 21 percent jump was proposed from fiscal 1981 to fiscal 1982. Between fiscal 1978 and 1981 the total NASA authorization had increased only from $4.1 billion to $5.5 billion.[35]

The Carter administration did continue to support the completion of three major programs inherited from the Ford administration: the space telescope, the Galileo mission to Jupiter (which was stretched out and delayed), and the LANDSAT-D satellite. The Carter

34. Public Papers, *Carter*, p. 536.

35. *AAAS Report, 1978*, p. 58; *AAAS Report, 1981*, p. 144; *AAAS Report, 1982*, pp. 14–15, 60–62; John Noble Wilford, "At NASA, All That's Up Is the Columbia," *New York Times*, November 1, 1981; idem, "Space Agency Sees Time of Sacrifice," *New York Times*, September 20, 1981.

administration was forced by budgetary pressures to delay committing itself to new projects and to stretch out the completion of others that had been introduced, but it did support a series of new programs for NASA in space sciences and space application. In space sciences, these included the International Solar Polar mission to study the sun (fiscal 1979); the Gamma Ray Observatory to observe gamma rays emanating from distant celestial objects (fiscal 1981); and the Venus Orbiting Imaging Radar satellite to map Venus by radar (fiscal 1982). In space applications, new programs included the multiagency AGRISTARS project, a remote sensing experiment to improve agricultural and resources assessment capabilities from space (fiscal 1980) and the National Oceanic Satellite System (NOSS) to analyze sea and ice conditions, marine weather, and marine pollution (fiscal 1981).[36]

Defense. Carter's fiscal 1978 amendments to President Ford's budget reflected a theme that he had stressed during the 1976 campaign: that the defense budget could be substantially cut without impairing national security. During the campaign, Carter had pledged to cut $5–7 billion from the Defense Department budget. In the amended fiscal 1978 budget, he in fact cut some $2.7 billion from Ford's defense authorization.

Defense R & D programs were less affected, suffering only a 2 percent cut from the 6 percent increase projected by the Ford administration. For fiscal years 1979 and 1980, the Carter administration proposed modest increases in defense R & D expenditures.[37]

Beginning in fiscal 1981, however, there was a dramatic turnaround in the Carter administration's willingness to shift priorities and commit substantial new resources to defense R & D. This turnabout stemmed from two sources: first, a growing perception that since the mid-1960s constricted Defense Department budgets had resulted in an erosion of the nation's defense, particularly in its technological superiority; and second, a heightened sense of urgency in defense by late 1979 because of events in Iran and Afghanistan.

President Carter, therefore, proposed substantial increases in the defense R & D budget of 21 and 22 percent in fiscal years 1981 and 1982, respectively. In the first two years of the Carter administration,

36. *OMB Special Analysis, 1978,* pp. 302–3; *OMB Special Analysis, 1979,* pp. 317–19; *OMB Special Analysis, 1980,* pp. 309–11; *OMB Special Analysis, 1981,* pp. 318–21; and *OMB Special Analysis, 1982,* pp. 317–19. For more detail on the rationale behind the funding decisions for NASA, also see the *AAAS Reports* for fiscal years 1978–1982 of the Carter administration.

37. *AAAS Report, 1978,* pp. 44–45.

defense R & D programs received about 45 percent of the total federal R & D funds. They received 48 percent of the total by fiscal 1982 in the last budget submitted by Carter.[38]

Perry valedictory. As the Carter administration left office, the valedictory statement of William J. Perry, under secretary of defense for research and engineering and the top defense R & D official, could well have been written by the Ford administration. It indeed formed a fitting preface to much that would be argued by Reagan administration officials.[39]

Perry opened his examination of the four Carter years with a review of the challenge and competition from the Soviet Union. "The 1980s," he said, "threaten to be a period of growing international tension and danger for the U.S. if the Soviet Union continues its military buildup and its aggressive attempts to expand political influence." Perry noted with concern that the Soviet Union was "outinvesting us by about a 2:1 margin" in total defense expenditures, "outproducing us by more than 2:1 in most categories of military equipment," and "now has about twice as great an effort as we have in military research and development."

Perry said that to counter these trends the United States would continue exploiting the fact that it had the "greatest technological capability and the strongest industrial base in the world." The key to any "investment strategy," then, was for the United States

> to *offset* the Soviet advantage in numbers by applying technology to equip our forces with weapons that outperform their Soviet counterpart. Fundamental to this strategy is the fact that the United States is five to ten years ahead of the Soviets in many of the basic technologies (for example, microelectronics, computers, and jet engines) most critical to our advanced weapons.

Perry went on to describe and analyze six areas of priority for defense R & D and acquisition:

Strategic modernization—decisions regarding cruise missile augmentation and deployment on B-52 bombers, full-scale development of the MX missile, and full-scale development of the Trident submarine and the long-range Trident missile

---

38. National Science Foundation, *Federal R & D Funding by Budget Function: Fiscal Years 1980–82* (Washington, D.C., 1981), pp. 5–8; National Science Foundation, *National Patterns of Science and Technology Resources: 1981* (Washington, D.C.: 1981), p. 29; *AAAS Report, 1982*, pp. 49–50.

39. The material in this section is from Department of Defense, "The FY 1982

Improved capability for rapid deployment forces—planning for a larger air transport plane, the CX, and for new equipment designed for light armored forces

Improved antiarmor capability—design and development of third-generation antiarmor precision guided artillery projectiles and production of a new second generation of laser-guided weapons

Maintenance of air superiority—programs to improve the capability of existing planes (F-4, F-5, and F-16) by improving firepower (AMRAAM missile), programs to improve tactical information systems through advanced surveillance equipment, and the design and development of the radar-evading Stealth airplane for the 1990s

Maintenance of naval superiority—major programs to upgrade anti-submarine capability, particularly development of passive acoustic systems to detect submarines at very long ranges and to improve anti–air warfare capability through more advanced, defensive ship-launched missiles

Technology base—maintenance of the health of the defense technology base, which had also been an area of concern and priority during the Ford administration

The technology base for defense R & D budget subcategories includes areas designated as research, exploratory development, and advanced technology development, and they constitute the areas of most advanced research and development. In the Carter fiscal 1981 budget, they made up $3.2 billion of the total $16.5 billion defense R & D budget allotment.[40]

The Carter administration, like the Ford administration, sought to achieve an annual real growth rate of 10 percent for research and 5 percent for advanced technology until the purchasing power of the mid-1960s had been restored. Perry noted that cuts by Congress during the first two years of the Carter administration had blocked this goal but that in the most recent budgets the increases of 10 and 5 percent had been achieved. The Carter fiscal 1982 budget proposed a 9 percent increase for defense research and technology. Among the important long-term initiatives were:

- very high speed integrated circuits (for use in precision guided missiles and submarine detection systems)
- directed energy (high-energy laser and particle beams)

Department of Defense Program for Research, Development, and Acquisition," statement by William J. Perry, under secretary of defense for research and engineering, to the 97th Congress, 1st session, January 20, 1981.

40. National Science Foundation, *Federal R & D Funding*, p. 6.

- advanced composite materials (allowing weight reduction and substitution for scarce critical materials such as chromium, titanium, and cobalt)
- manufacturing technology (improved production technology and computer-aided inspection systems for weapon system development)
- embedded computer software technology (the use of new software language to complement the rapid progress in computer hardware)[41]

Industrial Innovation. The years of the Carter administration coincided with a period of sharply rising concern about the state of the U.S. economy and the ability of the United States to compete economically in the world. Low productivity and slow growth, persistent inflation, and the continuing difficulties of such basic industries as automobiles and steel caused a number of politicians and economists to search for programs and policies to improve the nation's economic performance.

Out of this concern came a good deal of discussion about the need to reindustrialize America and a concomitant necessity for a new partnership between the government and the private sector. From Governor Jerry Brown of California on the left, who had stressed this theme in his 1976 presidential campaign, to *Business Week* on the right, which devoted many pages to reindustrialization schemes, came pressure for new policies.

In the Carter administration, the search for new policies and a new partnership was focused in two centers: the Commerce Department and the office of the president's science adviser, Frank Press. Press recalled in an interview:

> My recommendation to the president that we go forward with a major study initiative in the area of industrial innovation stemmed from a series of meetings I held with a number of business leaders from technology-intensive companies. There were remarkably similar points and themes which came out of these meetings about what the government should stop doing—that is, government policies that impeded industrial innovation—and what the government should start doing to foster such innovation.[42]

On the recommendation of the Commerce Department and his

41. Department of Defense, "FY 1982 Department of Defense Program," pp. 26–29.
42. Interview with Frank Press, president, National Academy of Sciences, September 22, 1981.

science adviser, President Carter directed early in 1978 that a full-scale domestic policy review on industrial innovation, headed by the Commerce Department, be undertaken. This review lasted some eighteen months and involved more than twenty government agencies and hundreds of outside organizations and individuals. Seven task forces, each with an external advisory committee, were established for the following areas: procurement; regulation of industry structure and competition; direct support for R & D; environmental, health, and safety regulations; economic and trade policy; patents; and information. The review was scheduled to be concluded by the spring of 1979, but the timetable slipped. The results were not published until October 1979, at which time Carter sent a special message on industrial innovation to Congress.

Among the initiatives he announced were:

- creation of a new Center for Utilization of Federal Technology as part of the Commerce Department's National Technical Information Service to facilitate the transfer of information
- establishment of five-year forecasts by federal health, safety, and environmental agencies of their "priorities and concerns" to allow industry time to develop compliance technologies
- creation of a Labor-Technology Forecasting System to develop advance warning of industrial change and permit timely adjustments
- issuance by the Justice Department of a statement clarifying its position regarding collaboration among research firms
- legislation to establish a uniform patent policy for government-sponsored research
- removal of barriers that inhibit the government in purchasing innovative products

Several new programs and institutions were also created:

- As authorized under the Stevenson-Wydler Technology Innovation Act (Public Law 96-480), four "generic technology" centers were to be established at a university or nongovernmental site, financed jointly by industry and the federal government. The centers would undertake research and development of technologies with special benefit for industry, specifically "generic technologies" that underlie many industrial activities such as welding, joining, robotics, corrosion prevention, powder metallurgy, and tribology (means of easing friction).
- Several state and regional Corporations for Industrial Development were to assist in starting up firms to develop and bring to market high-rise innovations, to provide guidance and management

advice to these firms, and to act as recipients of economic development assistance funds for the state or region.

• An existing National Science Foundation program—the Small Business Innovation Research Program—was to be expanded to foster university–small business technology projects.[43]

In fiscal 1980, the Carter administration began two major government-industry-university programs independent of the industrial innovation initiatives. It later cited them as models for future joint public–private sector activities.

The first was the Cooperative Automobile Research Program (CARP), a joint government-industry-university effort to undertake basic long-range research aimed at producing cars in the 1990s that would be more economical to manufacture and operate, attain greater fuel efficiency and safety, and reduce pollution. (CARP was also a direct response to Secretary of Transportation Brock Adams's call for an effort to reinvent the automobile.) All five major automobile manufacturers agreed to participate, and it was stipulated that government and industry would separately select and manage research projects. The research was to be carried out at universities as well as at private and government research laboratories. Combustion, structural mechanics, electrochemistry, tribology, material sciences, and catalysis were targeted for investigation.

It was initially agreed that for five years the automobile industry would match dollar for dollar the federal share of a ceiling of $100 million. Because of the condition of the industry, however, the 1981 contribution was waived.[44]

The second joint public-private program was the Ocean Margin Drilling Program, a joint venture among the government, the oil industry, and universities to study the geology of the world's ocean margins that lie just beyond the outer continental shelves. These ocean margins constitute one of the last unexplored areas on earth, and their potential for large oil and gas resources may be significant.

Under the program, ten oil companies, a number of universities, and the NSF would select and explore ten candidate sites for exploration. The total cost of a full ten-year effort was estimated at $800 million, to which the federal government and industry would contribute equally.[45]

43. Public Papers, *Carter*, pp. 2068–74; Press, "Science and Technology," pp. 143–44; *AAAS Report, 1981*, pp. 81–82.

44. Press, "Science and Technology," p. 144; White House, *America's New Beginning: A Program for Economic Recovery* (Washington, D.C., 1981), pp. 4–35; *AAAS Colloquium, 1980*, pp. 21–22.

45. Press, "Science and Technology," p. 144; "Research News," *Science*, February 8, 1980, pp. 627–28.

Regulatory and tax reform. Two other areas that were spotlighted as having a major effect on industrial innovation were government regulatory policy and government tax policy.

Carter administration officials found in discussion with industry leaders that one of the most persistent themes voiced was the deleterious effect that federal environmental, safety, and health regulations had on industrial innovation. Administration officials conceded that often there were important scientific judgments to make in achieving the regulatory goals, particularly in air and water pollution, hazardous waste disposal, toxic substances, occupational health and safety, and nuclear power.

The Carter administration took a number of steps to reduce unnecessary regulation. These included the creation of a regulatory council to oversee and monitor the full scope of federal regulations, publication of a regulatory calendar to provide a complete rundown on the government's major regulatory activities, establishment in the White House of a regulatory analysis review group to improve the scientific and economic basis of regulations, and promulgation of an executive order directing regulatory agencies to publish analyses backing up their regulations so that government officials and the public would be informed about the costs and benefits of individual regulations. In addition, Press took the lead in focusing federal agencies' attention and resources on the need to improve the quality of scientific data and analysis used in the regulatory process.[46]

In regard to tax incentives for industrial innovation, the Carter 1979 message to Congress was notable for its lack of recommendations. The president stated at the time, however, that "while [he] fully appreciate[d] that changing certain of our tax laws could provide additional incentives for investments in innovation," he thought that "such changes should not be viewed in isolation from other aspects of the economy." Carter said he would review such proposals for fiscal 1981. In August 1980, during the presidential campaign, he recommended an accelerated depreciation schedule for business taxes to encourage investment in new plant and equipment. At the same time, Press fought for a separate R & D tax credit, but the administration did not propose one.[47]

Proper government role. The Carter administration's effort to institute new or revised policies to enhance industrial innovation and thus improve U.S. competitiveness raised anew major questions about the necessary and proper role of the federal government. Rea-

46. Public Papers, *Carter,* pp. 2072–73; Press, "Science and Technology," pp. 144–45.
47. Public Papers, *Carter,* p. 2073; Press, "Science and Technology," pp. 143–44.

gan administration officials in 1981 would point to the Carter administration's industrial innovation initiatives as a contrast with their very different views about government–private sector division of responsibilities. In truth, however, the Carter administration was never of one mind on the subject.

There was a general consensus within the Carter administration that public and private R & D investment was connected in important ways to innovation, which in turn enhanced productivity and economic growth. Beyond these general precepts, however, were various shades of opinion about the actual gravity of the problem and about the steps that must be taken—particularly by the federal government—to correct it.

In his remarks announcing the industrial innovation initiatives program in 1979, President Carter said that the initiatives were intended to "restore what we have *begun to lose in a very serious fashion*, and that is the innovative nature of the American free enterprise system" [italics added]. To remedy this erosion, he proposed the formation of a "very close partnership with the different elements of American society, particularly in the private sector" to "rally cooperative efforts to spur industrial growth."[48]

At about the same time, however, the Carter administration's economic and science advisers were raising questions about the seriousness of the innovation problem and the public sector's influence on declining productivity. The 1979 *Economic Report of the President*, for example, said that most of the decline in federal R & D spending over the past decade had been in defense and space, which had less direct effect on productivity than either basic research or industry research. The report went on to suggest that more important than the decline in federal R & D support over the last ten years in explaining lower productivity was the shift in industry away from support of basic research and new product development.[49]

Similarly, the 1978 congressionally mandated *Science and Technology Report* contradicted a general perception that decreased R & D investment was leading to an erosion of the U.S. technological base. The report concluded:

> With regard to technology output and international earnings from R & D intensive activities, available data indicate little or no erosion in U.S. technological capabilities. The data on both inputs to and outputs from innovative activity thus

48. Public Papers, *Carter*, pp. 2068–69.
49. *Economic Report of the President* (1979), pp. 66–72.

suggest that the relationships between science and technology and economic and trade performance are not direct or simple. Neither the available economic nor technical indicators provide hard evidence of negative economic consequences.[50]

In contrast to this relaxed attitude, Commerce Department officials continued to stress the negative consequences of the decline in R & D investment as a percentage of GNP and decried this decline in comparison with the higher percentages that were being invested by several of America's major competitors. There were allusions to Japan, Inc., and suggestions that R & D and federal investment policy in the future should be targeted to backing the so-called high-technology winners that would provide the muscle for U.S. competitiveness in the world market.

Very little of the activist thinking in the Commerce Department was translated into policy or programs. As a result of the industrial initiatives effort, the Carter administration took steps to put into place four centers to undertake research on so-called generic technologies, which underlie many industrial activities. The administration also moved to establish a number of state and regional corporations for industrial development to assist firms in developing and marketing high-risk innovations and products. In neither instance, however, did the Carter administration envision a major effort or the commitment of large amounts of federal money. In a symbolic sense, the cooperative automobile research programs and the ocean margin drilling programs—which constituted direct government ties with specific industries— might in the long run have proved more important.

Reaction of Frank Press. In an interview, Press, the presidential science adviser, retrospectively reflected on the "limited goals" of the industrial innovation initiatives. He said that "some of the more grandiose ideas" of the Commerce Department did have a "kind of corporate statism tinge" but that such ideas "never developed much support in the White House."[51] Press said that President Carter's specific recommendations did not include big new joint public-private technology projects, nor did they lay the underpinning for stepped-up federal activity at the demonstration, development, and commercialization end of the R & D spectrum. Press, however, strongly defended the CARP and ocean margin drilling programs:

50. National Science Foundation, *Science and Technology Report (1978)* (Washington, D.C., 1978), p. 84.
51. The quotations from Press in this section are from an interview with the author on September 22, 1981.

These programs represented no great change in the underlying rationale for the use of federal funds. In both cases, the public resources would have been used for advanced or basic science and engineering. It was an attempt on our part to create new opportunities for the basic research community in the universities to make important contributions to vital industries. . . .

The experiments that were contemplated in CARP were such things as the basic characteristics of fuel combustion, aerodynamic properties of different automobile designs, and basic research in materials that might be used in automobiles, materials that were lighter and/or more durable. They represented research areas too far removed from application for the automobile companies to undertake them. In no sense were they aimed at actual product development (though the companies might have followed through in this regard), and thus they were also far removed from any intrusion on market or commercial judgments.

In conclusion, Press noted that there was ample precedent for the joint work contemplated in CARP and the ocean margin drilling. The federal government, he argued, had long undertaken much the same activity in aviation and indeed had often gone much further in that field in the direction of applied research and demonstration. He said:

One of the great strengths of the American aviation industry has been the long collaborative history with the government. The old NACA [National Advisory Council on Aeronautics] pioneered in airplane design and in the development of advanced engines—particularly the development and introduction of jet engines. There is a legitimate public role, I would contend, in sponsoring basic generic research and engineering projects.

3
Reagan Science and Technology Policy

The inauguration of Ronald Reagan in January 1981 heralded the arrival of a new governing philosophy—a new political and economic synthesis—for the nation. Just as in the 1930s, when the New Deal had combined loosely and erratically applied Keynesian economic theories with activist political theories of the role of government, so too did the Reagan administration seek to unite the sometimes disparate elements of "supply side" economic theory with a political philosophy propounding a much more constricted role of government.

Potential internal contradictions emerged in the administration's economic theories in 1981, but three essential elements continued to form the basic policies: tax reduction, regulatory reform, and limitations on the rate of increase in federal government spending. These economic initiatives were buttressed by President Reagan's strongly held political belief that government at all levels in the United States—particularly the federal government—had intervened too obtrusively in the lives of private citizens and that a scaling back of government activities should be a priority of the administration. The new governing philosophy had a direct effect on all federal programs—including the federal science and technology support system.

Economic Policy and R & D

The formulation and articulation of science and technology policy per se was not a priority during the first months of the Reagan administration. Most of the administration's attention was devoted to reshaping national economic policy. Research and development (R & D) programs, along with all other federal policies and programs, were inevitably evaluated through this prism. Speaking before the sixth annual American Association for the Advancement of Science (AAAS) R & D policy colloquium in June 1981, President Reagan's science adviser, George A. Keyworth, laid out the administration's view of the economic matrix from which R & D policy would emerge:

For perhaps too many years we have been emphasizing the distribution of the country's wealth far more than the improved production of it. Inflation has skyrocketed as our consumption has increased and our rate of savings declined. We have neglected necessary capital formation, investment in new more efficient productive plants, and longer range research and development. Our ever-increasing taxes have acted to drain off investment and dampen incentive and innovation. And, in our zeal to manage the many environmental, health and safety impacts of industrialization, we have often overreacted—or reacted without adequate knowledge—burdening many sectors of the society with unnecessary, costly regulation. The results have been slower industrial growth, a leveling off of productivity gains, and decreased competitiveness abroad.[1]

In a later speech, Keyworth said that to reverse these trends President Reagan was calling for major redirections in federal economic policies. Of the important new policies that will have a direct effect on R & D, he said:

First, and perhaps foremost, is the president's philosophy that the nation's future rests on an expanding economy spearheaded by new industrial investment and growth. One of the keys to achieving this [growth] are tax measures that will encourage savings and so provide a new flow of capital to industry. . . . Among these are the 25 percent tax credit for various research related expenditures, depreciation allowances that affect equipment purchases, and increased deductions for donations of scientific research equipment to colleges or universities. . . . Complementary administration efforts to remove disincentives to industrial research and innovation are focused primarily on reducing, and eventually eliminating, the excessive rules and regulations that in recent years have grown to sap so much of industry's resources. . . . [Finally] severe budget restraint [is the third key economic policy of the new administration]. . . . We are faced with the difficulty of operating during a time of severe budget restraint. While the President recognizes the importance of R & D to the economy, he is also committed to carrying out budget cuts that must be shared across the board by most federal agencies.[2]

1. Albert H. Teich et al., eds., *R & D and the New National Agenda: Federal R & D; Issues in Defense R & D; Agency Perspectives; R & D in the FY 1982 Budget: Impacts* (Washington, D.C.: American Association for the Advancement of Science, 1981), p. 138 (hereafter cited as *AAAS Colloquium, 1981*).

2. George A. Keyworth, director, Office of Science and Technology Policy, speech delivered before the Industrial Research Institute, Nashville, Tennessee, October 12, 1981.

Thus budget restraint formed the framework of the total federal R & D effort, and the tax and regulatory reform programs had elements directly aimed at unleashing and promoting private sector R & D, a goal that became the centerpiece of Reagan science policy.

Political Philosophy. The administration's economic initiatives were directly linked to firmly held views on the need for a sharply restricted role of government. In his first economic message to Congress, President Reagan said: "The goal of this administration is to nurture the strength and vitality of the American people by reducing the burdensome, intrusive role of the federal government. . . . It is our belief that only by reducing the growth of government can we increase the growth of the economy."[3]

Glenn R. Schleede, executive associate director of the Office of Management and Budget (OMB) in 1981, later explained the meaning of the new governing philosophy for federal science and technology policy: "Other administrations have declared that they would restrict the role of the federal government and not overtake activities properly belonging to the private sector. But the Reagan administration, I think you will see, will be the first actually to exercise this kind of restraint in any meaningful way."[4]

Overall Rationale

Reagan administration officials accepted the basic premises of earlier administrations regarding the contributions of science and technology to the welfare of the nation. Like the Ford and Carter administration officials, they stressed the connection between technological advance and economic growth and showed an understanding that many of the nation's problems—in energy, in the environment, and in transportation, for example—had large scientific and technological components.

Thus Murray L. Weidenbaum, chairman of the Council of Economic Advisers (1981–1982), told the June 1981 AAAS R & D colloquium:

> The President and his administration are well aware of the importance of R & D to our economic growth. As an economist, I focus on the importance of R & D as a key element in our dramatic slowdown in productivity in recent years. . . .

3. The White House, *America's New Beginning: A Program for Economic Recovery* (1981), p. 1.

4. Interview by author with Glenn R. Schleede, executive associate director of the Office of Management and Budget, September 9, 1981. (Schleede resigned from his position at the OMB on December 31, 1981.)

This is not simply a dry economic statistic. The problem of productivity growth is closely linked to trends in the profitability and competitiveness of American industry at home and abroad.[5]

In regard to the technological underpinning of many national security and domestic problems, Keyworth said:

Science is a critical factor in determining our ability and readiness to meet [these] problems. . . . No one can tell at this time what all the problems of our society will be. But we can be sure that many of them will be inextricably tied to science, and that our future problem-solving capability will depend on the depth and breadth of our scientific knowledge.[6]

Science and technology, then, were perceived as tools to achieve certain national goals. Keyworth said:

I would like to emphasize that we perceive R & D as a means to achieve necessary national objectives. . . . Science policy is not made in a vacuum. It is an exercise in priority-setting and decision making that must be carried out in the context of other national policies, such as those concerning national security, international relations, energy, social services, and the economy.[7]

The Role of Government. The overall commitment of the Reagan administration to limit and define more narrowly the role of the federal government in many areas was also seen in the shaping of science and technology policy. In the most complete statement up to that time on the Reagan administration's science policy, George Keyworth told the House Committee on Science and Technology on December 10, 1981, that the "federal role in science and technology must be different from that which has prevailed since World War II." It must, he said, be "appropriate to the 1980s—appropriate to a national mood which calls for increased vigor and acceptance of responsibility by individuals and organizations in the private sector and decreased involvement by the federal government in many of our affairs."[8]

5. *AAAS Colloquium, 1981*, p. 23.

6. George A. Keyworth, director, Office of Science and Technology Policy, testimony before the House Committee on Science and Technology, December 10, 1981 (hereafter cited as Keyworth, House science committee testimony).

7. Ibid.

8. Ibid.

Schleede, executive associate director of the OMB, spoke in an interview of the major changes by the Reagan administration in science policy in comparison with the Carter administration:

> By far the most important change came from this administration's redefinition of the federal role. In the R & D spectrum, stretching from the most esoteric basic research out through the actual commercialization of a technology, we have drawn the line for federal intervention and support back much farther toward the basic research end. In the civilian or domestic sector, we do not think the government should be funding demonstration, product development, and commercialization efforts.[9]

Schleede—who had also exercised science policy responsibilities in the Ford White House—went on to explain more fully both the continuities and the revisions instituted by the Reagan administration regarding the overall rationale for federal R & D support. Like the Carter and Ford administrations, he said, the Reagan administration acknowledged a predominant federal role in areas such as defense and space, where the federal government itself was the primary user of the end product. The federal government also retained large responsibilities for support of basic and applied research in a few areas such as health and agriculture, where there were broad societal benefits. Beyond this, Schleede said, "in contrast to earlier administrations, we begin to take a very skeptical and negative view" about the necessity of federal intervention and the expenditure of federal resources. "It is true," he said, "that we have acknowledged a commitment to fund demonstrations of long-range, high-risk, high-payoff technologies, but to the degree that the political realities will allow it, they will be very few and far between."[10]

To Schleede and other Reagan administration officials, the issue of central planning and bureaucratic dictation was important (on this point they echoed the warnings of outside conservative commentators, such as Simon Rottenberg and the Heritage Foundation (see appendix B). In a speech to the AAAS R & D policy colloquium in June 1981, Schleede opposed overambitious federal intervention:

> Many past R & D efforts in the civilian sector focused on what federal decision makers in Washington believed needed to be done in the national interest—not necessarily on what actually needed to be done. Adding money in the budget for R & D became a way of avoiding hard decisions.

9. Schleede interview.
10. Ibid.

Past efforts have focused too much on large federal investments to support federally selected technologies and federally selected goals, such as so many quads of energy from solar, synthetic or alcohol fuels—regardless of the economics involved.

Ironically, these federal projects funded from tax dollars were using the very capital that industry would need to fund their own technology ideas to meet their needs as they see them. When the President's program is in place, industry will have more capital and greater incentives to make needed R & D investment themselves, tailored to their own markets and corporate strategies, without need of federal subsidy.[11]

Budget, Resource Allocation. Two themes often stressed in 1981 by Reagan administration officials, particularly by the White House science adviser, Keyworth, were that although research would be protected, the next years would not be a time of growth and that it was therefore imperative that the federal science resource allocation system be honed to greater efficiency in the future. In his December 1981 testimony before the House science committee, Keyworth said, "We must now face up to difficult choices because we know federal expenditures for science cannot and will not continue to grow the way they have in the previous three decades."[12]

The public acceptance of a steady state or period of decline in public science support was a departure from the rhetoric if not the practices of the previous administrations. Both the Ford and the Carter administrations aimed for real annual increases in federal R & D (particularly basic research) to offset the substantial decline in federal R & D spending in the late 1960s to mid-1970s. Those previous administrations in practice had found this commitment difficult to sustain, but neither had backed away from the goal.

Keyworth challenged the idea that past growth for science had always produced beneficial results. He said in regard to past increases in federal R & D spending: "Throwing money at problems has not proven to be an effective strategy. In fact, it has often been responsible for furthering mediocrity rather than stimulating excellence."[13] In an interview in which he made much the same point, Keyworth added:

American science is still the best in the world, and I don't mean this as some kind of broadside attack. But the fact remains that there is a good deal of mediocre science in the

11. *AAAS Colloquium, 1981,* pp. 34–35.
12. Keyworth, House science committee testimony, December 10, 1981.
13. Ibid.

universities and in the national labs, and part of the blame must go to situations where there was more than enough money but not enough hard-nosed discrimination about priorities.[14]

Keyworth argued that the "first order of business" for the administration in fashioning a science policy was the "establishment of priorities not only within but across scientific disciplines. My central premise is simply that we cannot continue to distribute our limited support of research and development without applying stringent and fundamental criteria."[15]

In a number of speeches during the summer and fall of 1981, Keyworth outlined two basic criteria for the selection of projects: excellence and pertinence. Of excellence, he said: "Excellence should be the basis by which one judges the quality of science—the excellence of investigators, the excellence of the field." Of pertinence, he said: "An additional criterion for the support of areas of [applied] research directed toward technology advance is pertinence—and this means pertinence to the recognizable economic and social needs of the nation."[16]

In discussing the need to set rigorous priorities in a time of fiscal restraint, Keyworth attacked what he considered a misguided goal of U.S. science policy: to be preeminent in all scientific fields. He argued:

> There are a number of good reasons why we cannot expect to be preeminent in all scientific fields, nor is it necessarily desirable. The idea that we can't be first across the spectrum of science and technology is not simply a function of our current economic situation. The fact is that after World War II this country was alone in developing and pursuing technology. Since then the rest of the world has been catching up—with much help from us. Japan and Western Europe have achieved technological competitiveness, if not parity. This is healthy for the world and for its stability. . . . However, it follows that, because of the diversity inherent in industrial democracies, there are certain areas of science and technology that are more pertinent to other countries than to us. It is in these areas that others will attempt to be world leaders. But, there are other areas where the U.S. is leader and must remain so. This realization does not represent either a defeat-

14. Interview by author with George A. Keyworth, director, Office of Science and Technology Policy, September 16, 1981.

15. *AAAS Colloquium, 1981*, p. 142.

16. George A. Keyworth, director, Office of Science and Technology Policy, address delivered at the Lawrence Berkeley Laboratory, Oakland, California, October 3, 1981.

43

ist attitude or a lack of confidence in American scientists and engineers. Rather it is a recognition of the realities of today's competitive world. This recognition leads to the conclusion that, in science and technology, as in all endeavors, available resources must be identified, comparative advantages assessed, tough choices made, and priorities established, before resources are allocated.[17]

The creation of priorities among and within scientific disciplines would inevitably result in winners and losers, at least relatively. Keyworth accepted this as necessary in a time of fiscal stringency, because "we can no longer afford [the] luxury [simply] of adding resources to the best research areas, but *not* [taking] money away from less productive research areas."[18]

Keyworth said he understood that the implementation of new priorities would be gradual and that it was necessary to avoid disruptive budgetary upheavals. He said, however, that over the next few budget cycles he wanted to

> identify perhaps 10 percent of research where the promise and opportunities seemed greatest and give them increased emphasis, while at the same time deemphasizing areas where the opportunities do not seem so plentiful and where the record in the past decade has not matched that of other fields.

He acknowledged that this would involve value judgments, but he argued that

> through a wide and thorough review process that involves peer and advisory groups, agency personnel, Congress, the OMB, and the White House science office, we can minimize parochial interests and evaluate realistically the best use for our limited research dollars.[19]

Basic Research. In their defense of the government's role in supporting basic scientific research, Reagan administration officials demonstrated a large degree of continuity with past administrations. They did not follow the recommendations of some of the more conservative voices outside the government, such as Milton Friedman (appendix B), and withdraw support from basic science.

17. George A. Keyworth, address delivered before the American Association for the Advancement of Science, Washington, D.C., January 3, 1982.

18. Ibid.

19. Keyworth interview.

Schleede of the OMB said, "I haven't seen any evidence that [Friedman's call to abolish the NSF and withdraw federal dollars from basic research] has any influence or following within the administration. On the contrary, like earlier Republican administrations, we tend to be softhearted about basic research; and there is a strongly protective streak in the OMB."[20]

The special place accorded basic research by the Reagan administration was signaled early. In April 1981, the OMB published a revised special analysis of the fiscal 1982 R & D budget, which reflected at least preliminary administration policy goals in basic research. It said:

> One area of traditional federal responsibility that has been protected from severe reductions in the revised 1982 budget is support of basic research. . . . Many believe that [the federal basic research] investment can be utilized most efficiently if it is accompanied by a measure of long-term stability in funding because basic research is a cumulative process, for example, gaps created in a period of reduced support cannot be quickly overcome by even a sharper increase in basic research spending at a later date. The revised 1982 budget continues to provide strong support for basic research.[21]

Weidenbaum, speaking to the AAAS R & D policy colloquium in June 1981, echoed the arguments of Ford and Carter administration economists:

> Economists are well aware that even in the most supportive environment most areas of basic research still require public support. From my professional perspective this is because basic research is so risky, and because the discoveries it may make are not easily converted to rewards for individual entrepreneurs. Any sensible policy towards science must recognize the essential role of basic research as the foundation of our economic progress, and the concomitant need to give it public as well as private financial support.[22]

In the December 1981 comprehensive statement on the Reagan administration's science policy, Keyworth said:

> Basic research warrants government support because it is an

20. Schleede interview.

21. Office of Management and Budget, "Revised Special Analysis of the R & D Component of the 1981 and 1982 Budgets of the U.S. Government," mimeographed (Washington, D.C., April 1981), p. 2.

22. *AAAS Colloquium, 1981*, pp. 24–25.

investment in the future—in a better quality of life, better security, a better economy, and simply better understanding. In addition to its general societal benefit, basic research is essential to the conduct of many activities, such as defense and space, for which the federal government has responsibility. It should thus be a component part of the research budgets of all government agencies whose missions depend upon a strong scientific and technological base.[23]

Keyworth also said that "because of the inherent uncertainty in its application, wide-ranging support across fields and subfields of science should be maintained, thus providing the country with a capability to take advantage of important breakthroughs quickly and to respond to changing needs." He noted, however, that basic research, like the rest of the public science support system, faced the need to establish priorities in a period of sustained budgetary constraint. He said that the United States could no longer expect to be number one in all basic scientific disciplines any more than it could expect to be number one in applied research or commercial production of all new technologies.

Keyworth rejected the use of external criteria to determine the adequacy of the federal investment in basic research. He said:

> Many have proposed tying support for basic research to some other factor, such as GNP, or assuring that there is some specified percent growth each year. I do not believe such an approach is wise, because it does not relate to the quality of the basic research itself. While decision making may not be easy, we should not derogate from our responsibility by adopting rules of thumb that tie the support of basic research to some rigid external factor.[24]

The rejection of an "external factor," such as a fixed percentage growth for basic research, was a substantial change from the Ford and Carter administrations, which held that because of the relative decline in support for basic research from the late 1960s to the mid-1970s, the federal goal for the foreseeable future should be annual increases that somewhat exceeded the rate of inflation.

Demonstration, Development, Commercialization. Reagan administration officials said their negative attitude toward government support of civilian demonstration and commercialization programs was a significant contrast with preceding administrations of both parties.

23. Keyworth, House science committee testimony, December 10, 1981.
24. Ibid.

OMB's Schleede vowed that the administration would "rigorously enforce" its stringent criteria for federal intervention beyond basic research support.[25] President Carter had defended federal underwriting of projects beyond basic and applied research "where there is a national need to accelerate the development of new technologies in the private sector" and when "the risk is great or the costs inordinately high, such as with many aspects of energy and transportation."[26]

Reagan administration officials directly challenged the assumptions of the acceleration argument and expressed misgivings about the uses of the high risk–high cost–high payoff argument. Schleede said, "The federal government has an abysmal record in choosing and bringing to the marketplace civilian technologies. One cannot think of a single technology that it has succeeded in accelerating . . . the process is just too complex for clumsy bureaucratic manipulation to manage successfully."[27]

In regard to the high risk–high cost–high payoff argument for funding demonstration and development programs, Frederick Khedouri, OMB associate director for natural resources, energy, and science, said: "There are a few areas where this argument is valid: the case of fusion R & D is the best example. But the problem is that the argument is often used to support projects that don't legitimately pass the criteria." Khedouri pointed to industry pressure and bureaucratic imperialism as sources of the problem. He said, "We know there's a lot of corporate socialism out there, just as there is the ordinary kind. Those industry guys are very sophisticated, and if you show them free dough, they're very adept at extracting it from the federal government."[28]

Khedouri said, however, that as a general proposition, government intervention at the demonstration and commercialization end of R & D had "pernicious results." He argued:

> Inevitably, the intrusion of federal dollars will have a displacement effect, both pulling private efforts in the direction of the technologies the bureaucrats have chosen and suppressing activities in other technologies. This is exactly what was happening in photovoltaics, where the Carter administration was actively engaged in product development and commercialization. That's why we want to get out—so that a truly competitive situation can reassert itself. It's also the

25. Schleede interview.

26. Public Papers of the Presidents, *Jimmy Carter (1979)*, pp. 529–30.

27. Schleede interview.

28. Interview by author with Frederick Khedouri, associate director for natural resources, energy, and science, OMB, September 11, 1981.

reason we want to cut back on synthetic fuels—where because of the huge sums involved, we were also heading for complete displacement of private sector and market judgments.[29]

Crosscurrents, Internal Conflicts. It is undoubtedly true, as an analysis of the revised fiscal 1982 budget shows, that the Reagan administration, more than previous administrations, has attempted to retrench from federal support of demonstration and commercialization projects. It is also true, however, that, like previous administrations, it has found that outside political pressures and internal disagreements have hampered the full accomplishment of these goals. The two most glaring contradictions to free-market purists in the administration are the continuing support of the hugely expensive synthetic fuels and breeder reactor demonstration programs. The Synthetic Fuels Corporation, which the administration originally had intended to kill but did not, will have at its disposal over $17 billion in the next four years to spend on demonstration and commercialization synthetic fuel projects. The Clinch River breeder reactor, on which just over $1 billion has been spent, is now projected to cost some $3.2 billion before completion later in the decade.[30]

Although science adviser Keyworth expressed "enthusiastic" support for the Clinch River project, OMB officials Schleede and Khedouri declined to express personal endorsements.[31] Khedouri said that "we can't be wholly pure" in carrying out the free-market tests and that in this case "political judgments" prevailed. Schleede said it was "very difficult to ask the president to stop a project that is under the personal protection of the Senate majority leader."[32] Senate Majority Leader Howard Baker (Republican, Tennessee) is the leading congressional supporter of the Clinch River project, which is being constructed in his home state.

In regard to synthetic fuels, Schleede predicted that even though the Reagan administration did not move to kill the Synthetic Fuels Corporation, it would "cut back substantially" on the synthetic fuels program and much of the $17 billion cache appropriated for the program would never be drawn upon. He explained the administration's position by noting that congressional support was very strong and that President Reagan had made a political judgment that other

29. Ibid.
30. For details, see chapter 4.
31. Khedouri interview; Schleede interview.
32. Schleede interview.

budget cuts were more important than those in synthetic fuels. In any case, these were off-budget expenses that did not have an effect on the current or future budget deficits. "We have to make these kinds of political trade-offs all the time," Schleede said.[33]

Innovation and Productivity

Like the Carter administration, the Reagan administration early on faced a series of policy questions regarding measures to increase productivity and restore economic growth and to facilitate innovation as a part of that strategy. Like the Carter administration, it was also forced to make policy judgments from limited data and from disagreements among economists on the implications of the data for public policy. Laid on top of this clouded economic judgmental base was the fact that the Reagan administration brought with it a very different political philosophy about the proper role of the federal government. Thus, though there were areas of policy agreement with the Carter administration (for example, patent and trust policy), there was substantial disagreement regarding the nature and specifics of government intervention to stimulate innovation and increase productivity.

R & D Productivity. There is a consensus among economists that innovation—the development of new and more efficient technologies and the application of both new and improved technologies by industry—is one of the most important determinants of productivity growth. There is not a consensus, however, on the relationship between national expenditures for R & D and increases and decreases in productivity. To oversimplify somewhat, one school, identified closely with the economist John W. Kendrick, holds that there is a strong, causal relationship between R & D and productivity. On June 13, 1978, Kendrick told the Joint Economic Committee:

> With respect to the proximate determinants of productivity increase, the fountainhead of advancing technological knowledge, the most important source of productivity, is research and development. In recent decades, it has been formal R & D outlays that have accounted for most of the increase in the stock of technological knowledge applied to productive processes.[34]

33. Ibid.
34. John W. Kendrick, testimony before the Joint Economic Committee, June 13, 1978.

Indirect evidence supports Kendrick's thesis. For example, the decline in the rate of productivity growth in the United States partially coincided with and partially followed a decline in the total R & D spending in the United States. Although the United States continued to spend more on R & D in absolute terms than our major trading partners, several of them—Japan and Germany, for example—have been increasing their R & D spending at a more rapid rate, in terms of GNP, than the United States has. Both Japan and Germany experienced higher productivity rates during the 1970s than the United States. Another indicator of innovation, though a crude one, is the number of patents granted per year. The number of patents granted to U.S. citizens has substantially declined since 1973, but the number of patents granted to foreigners has substantially increased since the late 1960s.

Researchers have found in comparing specific industries within the U.S. economy that there is a relationship between the amount spent on R & D and the rate of productivity growth and that within an industry variations of R & D spending influence productivity growth, though the amount, timing, and direction are uncertain. Further, several studies have concluded that the private economic returns to corporations that invest in R & D are higher than private returns on other investments—for example, at least as high as the returns from investments in buildings and equipment. (It might also be noted, incidentally, that two studies have concluded that the rates of return on R & D investment are higher for company-financed R & D than for R & D in which the federal government is involved.)[35]

Despite the substantial indirect evidence connecting R & D to productivity, another body of literature points to the complexity of the innovation process and holds that R & D spending is only one of a number of factors that influence increases or decreases in productivity. It maintains that there is little direct relationship between R & D spending, productivity, and economic growth. The work of the economist Edward Denison best represents the views of this group. Denison has produced several studies of factors influencing economic growth, which are regarded as classics in the field. In his *Accounting*

35. See Roger Brinner, *Technology, Labor, and Economic Potential* (Data Resources, Inc., 1978), chap. 1 and pp.. 95–100; Zvi Griliches, "R & D and the Productivity Slowdown," *American Economic Review* (May 1980), pp. 343–47; M. Ishaw Nadiri, "Sectoral Productivity Slowdown," *American Economic Review* (May 1980), pp. 349–52; Edwin Mansfield, "Federal Support of Research and Development Activities," in *Priorities and Efficiency in Federal Research and Development* (Joint Economic Committee, 1976); and Zvi Griliches, "Return to Research and Development Expenditures in the Private Sector," in J. W. Kendrick and B. N. Vaccara, eds., *New Developments in Productivity Measurement and Analysis* (University of Chicago Press, 1979), pp. 419–54.

for Slower Economic Growth, Denison attributes much of the recent decline of productivity to a slowdown in "advances in knowledge" or innovation:

> The contribution of advances in knowledge is, conceptually, a comprehensive measure of the gains in measured output that result from the incorporation of new knowledge of any type—managerial and organizational as well as technological—regardless of the source of that knowledge, the way it is transmitted to those who can make use of it, or the way it is incorporated into production.[36]

Although he says that the slowdown in "advances in knowledge" was significant in the recent decline in productivity in the United States, Denison doubts that reduced R & D spending was much of a factor. In support of this contention, he points out that a substantial part of R & D spending—particularly a large part of the decline from the late 1960s to the mid-1970s in federal R & D spending—is in defense, an area that has little effect on measured productivity. In the 1970s, while overall national R & D spending declined, industry R & D—which has had higher rates of return, according to several studies—actually increased. Denison concludes that only one-sixth of the total contribution of "advances in knowledge" is related to R & D spending.[37]

Whatever their views on the exact relationship between R & D and productivity, there is general agreement among economists that the process of innovation is complex and affected by a number of factors and government policies. At the most basic level, for example, most economists would agree that the overall state of the economy and expectations for inflation have major effects on innovation. Thus the Congressional Budget Office (CBO), in a study of the problem of productivity, concluded: "The general state of the economy is believed to be a major determinant of innovation. If the economic environment is favorable to investment and risk-taking, it is conducive to innovation."[38] CBO went on to pinpoint inflation as a major negative factor in relation to innovation:

> A good deal of circumstantial evidence suggests that the climate for innovation, and the prospective returns for R & D

36. Quoted in George N. Carlson, "Tax Policy toward Research and Development," *Technology in Society*, vol. 3, nos. 1 and 2 (1981), p. 69.

37. Ibid.

38. Congressional Budget Office, *The Productivity Problem: Alternatives for Action* (Washington, D.C., January 1981), p. 77. See also National Science Foundation, *Science and Technology Report (1978)* (Washington, D.C., 1978) pp. 57–86.

in particular, may have deteriorated during the 1970s. . . . Higher inflation may have added to uncertainty and caused businesses to curtail their R & D plans, especially for basic research which has a more delayed and uncertain payoff than many alternative investments.[39]

Lower investment and decreased capital formation—in addition to the unsettling effect of inflation—have been cited as significant drags on innovation, particularly during the 1970s. CBO said in the study just cited: "Another negative influence . . . was the depressed state of the capital markets during much of the 1970s. This was especially discouraging to the development of small, high-technology businesses."[40] The economist J. A. Tatom has said: "The relatively slow pace of capital formation, including research and development capital, has quietly played an important role in productivity decline."[41] Kendrick, who assigns a large role to R & D in causing productivity changes, argues for overall policies to stimulate investment:

> Policies to promote tangible investment . . . would obviously accelerate the growth of real product per unit of labor input. . . . In addition, the acceleration in tangible capital formation would have a positive effect on R & D spending and other tangible investments that are part and parcel of the inventive-innovation process.[42]

The impact of government regulations has also been increasingly pointed to as a deterrent to innovation:

> The regulatory impact [on] R & D is multifaceted. Regulation may extend the waiting time for a given return to be earned on investment. This is perhaps most obvious for drug and medical products which must pass lengthy government safety and effectiveness tests prior to release for the market. . . . In addition, regulation increases uncertainty. Firms are at the mercy of regulators who may have the capability to change regulations *ex post*, after firms have decided on a product or process mix, and after the optimal mix of inputs has been determined. Finally . . . regulations distort resource allocations away from R & D and all other traditional

39. Congressional Budget Office, *The Productivity Problem*, p. 77.

40. Ibid., p. 78.

41. Quoted in Carlson, "Tax Policy," p. 70.

42. John W. Kendrick, "Productivity Trends and the Recent Slowdown: Historical Perspective, Causal Factors, and Policy Options," *Contemporary Economic Problems* (Washington, D.C.: American Enterprise Institute, 1979), p. 51.

investments toward the direction of tasks dictated by regula-
tors.[43]

Both patent and trust policies exercise key influences on innovation. Shifts in their basic direction and philosophy can produce both
incentives and disincentives to produce new goods and services in
the economy.

Policies to Stimulate Innovation

The Reagan administration has undertaken a number of policies that
both indirectly and directly are aimed at stimulating innovation and
thereby increasing productivity and economic growth. In some cases
the administration has built on the experience and policies of the
Carter administration; in others it has either branched off in new
directions or completely reversed directions.

Trust, Patent, and Regulatory Policy. The Reagan administration has
either continued or expanded efforts begun in the Carter administration in trust, patent, and regulatory policy. In regard to trust policy
and joint efforts by firms to undertake R & D, the administration in
effect has continued the antitrust guide issued by the Carter administration for use by technical experts in industry, universities, and
government.

In patent policy, the administration is seeking to expand legislation enacted under President Carter to strengthen the incentives for
industrial R & D. That legislation made it easier for universities and
small businesses to take title to products and processes developed
under government contracts. The Reagan administration has endorsed this concept and is working with congressional committees to
enact legislation to extend this privilege to all corporations.[44]

Regulatory reform has become a central goal of the Reagan administration's domestic policy. Under the direction of Vice President
Bush, the President's Task Force on Regulatory Relief is reviewing
hundreds of existing economic and social regulations, with the aim of
abolishing or scaling down many of them. As a part of this process,
the White House science adviser, Keyworth, heads a working group
evaluating the scientific base of many of the regulations in health,
safety, and the environment. Further, the administration has indi-

---

43. Senator Lloyd Bentsen, "Taxation, Research, and Development," *Technology in
Society,* vol. 3, nos. 1 and 2 (1981), p. 28.
44. Keyworth, Nashville speech.

cated that in the future it will seek substantial changes in the underlying environmental, health, and safety statutes to further its deregulation goals.[45]

Economic Policy Options to Stimulate Innovation. There are two routes—one indirect and one direct—that the government could take to stimulate industrial innovation. Indirectly, it could rely heavily, if not exclusively, on taxes. This would include general personal and corporate tax reduction, liberal depreciation for plants and equipment, and targeted tax credits for various forms of R & D investment. A more direct route (which could also be used in conjunction with taxes) would be for the government to increase its direct outlays to private industry for R & D projects that increase productivity, to provide loans or price guarantees for innovative products or processes, and to establish new institutional mechanisms, such as the Carter administration's generic technology centers for public-private collaboration.

In addition to the economic arguments for and against the two routes, there are important political questions and implications about the proper role of government and the private sector.

Tax Options. The Reagan administration, because of its economic assumptions and its strong views on limited government, has opted solely for the indirect, tax policy route to spur innovation. The administration's original intention in the 1981 tax reform bill was to provide only general incentives to spur investment—including investment in R & D. Thus the administration supported a substantial reduction in personal income taxes to free money to encourage persons to invest individually, and it supported liberalized depreciation rules to induce industry to invest in plant and equipment. During negotiations on the tax bill, however, the administration accepted a provision for a 25 percent targeted tax credit on incremental spending for wages, materials, and supplies used for research and development. Thus the final tax package contained both general incentives for new capital investments (embodied in the personal tax cuts and new depreciation rules) and a specific incentive for private sector R & D spending, which cost the government less revenue.[46]

The 1981 tax bill passed by Congress reduced personal income taxes across the board by 25 percent over the next three years. The act

45. Ibid.

46. For an excellent analysis of the R & D aspects of the tax bill negotiations, see Colin Norman, "Is Reaganomics Good for Technology?" *Science*, August 21, 1981.

also lowered the capital gains, gift, and estate taxes. The liberalized depreciation rules allowed faster write-offs by corporations for plants and equipment: cars, trucks, and R & D equipment could be written off in three years, machinery in five years, and buildings in ten years. Together the tax cuts reduced personal and corporate taxes by an estimated $750 billion over the next five years. (The 1982 tax bill reduced the overall personal and business tax cuts to about $350 million over the next five years.) The administration also estimated that the aggregate investment incentives in the 1981 act would induce an additional $3 billion in R & D investment over the next five years, some $700 million of it stemming from the 25 percent R & D credit.[47]

The Reagan administration had only reluctantly accepted the 25 percent R & D tax credit during the negotiations on the tax bill. Administration officials would have preferred not to add the R & D tax credit for two reasons. First, the administration wanted a clean bill, limited to personal income tax cuts and liberal depreciation rules. Second, in general it opposed the targeted tax cuts in the R & D tax credit. One administration official said: "Once you start down the road of targeting, all kinds of interest groups will flood you with requests. In general, the administration—certainly the Council of Economic Advisers and the Treasury—opposes this kind of tax incentives."[48] Whatever the initial attitude toward the R & D tax credit, the administration later argued that the final tax package would give strong impetus to increased R & D investment and would ultimately spur innovation.

In a speech to the AAAS R & D policy colloquium in June 1981, CEA Chairman Murray Weidenbaum explained the rationale for both the personal and the corporate tax cuts and tied them to the administration's emerging R & D policies: The energy of the private sector "must be focused by provision of the proper incentive through changes in the tax code. . . . In the corporate sector this will be achieved primarily through encouraging investment. As you know, the principal means of achieving this is through the accelerated capital cost recovery—the now-famous 10-5-3 program." R & D, however, "is a special form of investment and . . . requires special encouragement," he said. The administration proposed to encourage R & D

47. George A. Keyworth, director, Office of Science and Technology Policy, Keynote Lecture, 148th Annual Meeting of the American Association for the Advancement of Science, Washington, D.C., January 3, 1982; Glenn L. Schleede, lecture, AAAS R & D Colloquium, Washington, D.C., June 25, 1981. Cost estimates for the targeted R & D tax credit were omitted from the printed version of the colloquium proceedings (*AAAS R & D Colloquium, 1981*).

48. Staff member, Council of Economic Advisers, interview, January 15, 1982.

investment in two ways: first, by granting R & D equipment more favorable treatment than other equipment (a tax life of three years as against five years for other equipment); and second, by allowing a 25 percent tax credit for incremental spending on wages and salaries of researchers.

Weidenbaum also said that the phased, three-year reductions in personal income taxes would stimulate industrial innovation. The goal of the personal income tax cut, he said, was to restore the incentives to work, save, and invest. Some had contended, he noted, that "such a program is too broad and therefore wrong."

> I am sure that each of you has in mind a project or group that you believe could better be financed out of tax savings. Many might argue that science itself, the research effort, space exploration, or industrial technology ought to be the recipients of the federal revenue forgone in this "untargeted" tax cut. But this administration has a different view. We believe the personal tax cuts are targeted. We believe that the most effective, targeted tax cut is one which provides the broad incentives for each person to do his or her best. . . . The essential need is to restore the incentive for creativity. . . . Rather than forcing economic growth through one government-selected channel or another, we believe that the people as a whole will invest their time, talents and wealth in the most productive activities—those which the signals of the competitive market indicate are likely to yield the highest returns.[49]

Public, private roles. The administration's decision to rely on taxes to increase investment in innovation indirectly was based on economic theories and political beliefs concerning the proper role of the federal government.

In his remarks to the AAAS R & D policy colloquium in June, Weidenbaum concluded:

> There is no question but that one of the critical elements in restoring our economy to healthy, sustained growth is a vigorous expansion of research and development activity. However, it should also be clear that, to this administration's way of thinking, expansion should take place in the private sector, financed in the main by private funds. . . . [The main role of the government is to] promote private sector research and development by providing a stable, competitive economic framework, in which investors and researchers will be

49. *AAAS R & D Colloquium, 1981*, p. 28.

more willing to make commitment to the always risky enterprise of R & D.[50]

The former OMB executive associate director Schleede said in an interview that the exclusive reliance on indirect incentives for innovation embodied in the administration's economic program is

a dramatic shift in the philosophy of the role of government. . . . The primary aim of the administration's program for [R & D] is to free up for the private sector the resources necessary to stimulate R & D investment and hence innovation. We think that centralized direction of R & D from the Executive Office of the President or from the cabinet departments contains so many inefficiencies—both political and economic—that the waste of resources is inevitably enormous. The innovation process is too complex for the government to attempt to control or direct it from Washington.[51]

Effect of the tax package. Administration officials have publicly claimed that the Economic Recovery Tax Act of 1981 will stimulate some $3 billion in corporate R & D spending over the next five years and that the R & D tax credit provision would account for about $700 million of this. OMB's Schleede has said, however, that these "are not hard figures and represent just our best guesses and estimates."[52]

Economists and industrial research executives are also uncertain about the ultimate effect of the new tax act on R & D spending, innovation, and productivity. Early in 1981, as the debate and negotiations over the tax bills were getting under way, the quarterly *Technology in Society* published a special issue entitled "Taxation, Technology, and the U.S. Economy," which consisted of policy papers from twenty-five leading experts in taxation, productivity, and innovation. The contributors included a group of professional economists, corporate research executives, venture capitalists, and government officials. In summary, the editors noted "an extraordinary degree of unanimity as to the urgency of the U.S. [economic] condition" and that "foremost among the remedial measures is tax policy."[53] Although there were various tax policy recommendations, the editors found that a majority of them centered on capital formation and investment and

50. Ibid., p. 29.
51. Schleede interview.
52. Ibid.
53. Ralph Landau and N. Bruce Hannay, "Taxation, Technology, and the U.S. Economy: Introduction and Overview," *Technology in Society*, vol. 3, nos. 1 and 2 (1981), pp. 16–17.

that accelerated depreciation was cited the most. R & D tax concessions, they found, also received wide support. There was no consensus on the personal income tax cuts. The editors concluded:

> In essence, then, our intuition is that there is a widespread consensus on the need for far-reaching business and investment tax measures to stimulate R & D capital formation. This view extends to tax reduction on capital gains and present high marginal rates on investment income. There is no real agreement on the extent of general personal income tax cuts, probably because the impact on technology and innovation is less direct.[54]

Two economists who contributed papers to the *Technology in Society* special issue were Dale W. Jorgenson of Harvard University and Joseph J. Cordes of George Washington University. Discussions with them after passage of the 1981 tax act revealed mixed feelings about its effects. Both economists said the targeted R & D tax credit would produce an increase in industry R & D spending, at least in the short run. Cordes said:

> The R & D tax credit is scheduled to run only until 1986. My guess is that corporations will move up their R & D funding schedules to take advantage of this provision; that is, a lot of research that might have to be done later in the decade will be moved up to take advantage of the tax breaks until 1986.

Cordes said, however, that one key group of corporations—small, high-technology firms—might not be able to take advantage of new tax incentives:

> A lot of innovation originates with these small, high-technology firms, and because of their low capitalization and small profit margins, the [R & D targeted tax credit] may not help them all that much. The way to have induced more R & D spending from these companies would have been to have made the tax credit refundable—which the tax act did not do.[55]

Both economists were uncertain about the effect of the new depreciation rules on innovation and productivity. Cordes said:

> To the degree that the tax package makes capital formation cheaper and thus produces more investment, there should be a positive effect on innovation—since innovation is often embedded in investment in new plants and equipment.

54. Ibid., p. 18.
55. Separate interviews by the author with Dale W. Jorgenson and Joseph J. Cordes, January 21, 1982.

Both Cordes and Jorgenson, however, noted that because of the skewed nature of the depreciation rules, the effect on productivity could be mixed. Jorgenson said:

> Optimally, the tax system should be neutral in relation to investment among business sectors. The new depreciation rules, however, are not neutral—indeed, I calculate that there is a difference of over 50 percent in the effective tax rates between industries that get the most advantage from the act (in this case, air transportation companies) and those industries which get the least (in this case, public utilities, other than gas and electric utilities). Thus I would expect that you might very well find increased productivity within particular industries but a drag on productivity among all industries because of the potential misallocation of resources stemming from the tax rate differential.[56]

Major dissent. There are economists who disagree with the approach of using the tax system to increase R & D spending and enhance productivity. On both economic and political grounds, for example, Joseph Pechman of the Brookings Institution has taken issue with the philosophy of the 1981 tax act. Speaking before the AAAS R & D policy colloquium in June 1980, Pechman opposed additional tax incentives for R & D:

> The tax law already provides full immediate deduction for research and development outlays. This is about as far as the tax law should go. If we are to spend federal funds to promote research and development, we should make an effort to maximize the return of our money. In general, tax deductions or tax credits are difficult to limit and usually turn out to be wasteful.[57]

In a later discussion, Pechman extended his remarks, saying he thought that some econometricians exaggerated the positive effect of tax incentives on investment and that the payoff was actually only "modest." In general, Pechman said, public subsidies for R & D should be provided by direct outlays and administered by the relevant federal science or technology agency that "can distinguish useful projects."[58]

Industry reaction. Interviews with executives of technology-based firms after passage of the tax reform act reveal a similar uncertainty about the effect of the depreciation capital gains and targeted R & D

---

56. Jorgenson interview; Cordes interview.
57. *AAAS R & D Colloquiun, 1980,* pp. 48–49.
58. Ibid., pp. 55–56.

tax revisions. Edward E. David, president of Exxon research and engineering and former (1971–1973) science adviser to President Nixon, said:

> It's really impossible to say how much new spending the R & D tax credit provision will generate. In my view, however, it's the total economic package that it is important to focus on. Corporations are much more likely to be swayed by the general direction of economic policy than by any of the particulars. And in that regard, I think the basic thrust of the president's economic policies will greatly stimulate more investment, particularly R & D investment.[59]

Lewis M. Branscomb, chairman of the National Science Board and vice president and chief scientist of IBM, generally supported the administration's tax policy, but doubted that the incremental R & D tax credit per se would have much effect. He said:

> The fact is that technology-based corporations like IBM have been steadily increasing their R & D investment over the past years, and because the tax credit is only for *incremental* increases, IBM and other corporations like it probably won't get much tax advantage out of it because we are already spending what we consider about the right amount on R & D.[60]

Branscomb's comments point up a situation that was little discussed during the tax debate: that is, that the perceived decline in R & D spending over the last decade has come almost entirely from a drop in federal R & D activities. The AAAS has calculated that from 1967 to 1981, industry-funded R & D increased by about 49 percent in real terms.[61] Thus, as Branscomb said, the R & D tax credits, which apply only to additional funds, may have only limited effect because there already has been substantial growth in industry-sponsored R & D.

In general, however, as David and Branscomb illustrate, whatever the individual judgment on the specific effect of the revised depreciation rules or the R & D tax credit, most executives of technology-based corporations say the tax bill is a good one. William O. Baker, the recently retired head of Bell Laboratories, said:

59. Interview by author with Edward E. David, president, Exxon research and engineering, September 17, 1981; also, Edward E. David, lecture, AAAS Mass Media Science Fellows, American Association for the Advancement of Science, Washington, D.C., June 3, 1981.

60. Interview by author with Lewis M. Branscomb, September 18, 1981.

61. Norman, "Is Reaganonomics Good for Technology?" p. 844.

It's an important step in the right direction—and to my mind the right direction is having the federal government concentrate direct funding on basic and long-term research, while allowing the private sector to keep the necessary resources to fund R & D leading to commercial products and new processes.[62]

Dismantlement of Carter Initiatives. The Reagan administration has emphatically rejected the more positive, direct government initiatives that emerged from President Carter's industrial innovation initiatives. As noted in chapter 2, the Carter administration moved only tentatively toward direct government support and collaboration with industry in innovation, and it did not commit large sums to these projects. Nevertheless, it had planned to increase fiscal 1982 funding for the generic technology centers and for the regional centers for innovation in the Office of Productivity Technology and Innovation, in the Commerce Department. It had also planned to increase substantially funding for the Cooperative Automobile Research Program (CARP), the joint government–automobile company initiative to undertake basic research aimed at developing more fuel-efficient cars in the 1990s. The National Science Foundation (NSF) had also established several similar joint university-government-corporate innovation programs. The Reagan administration eliminated the Commerce Department programs altogether and drastically reduced funding for the NSF programs.[63]

When asked the major differences in philosophy and programs between the research and development programs of the Carter and the Reagan administrations, the Reagan administration invariably cites industrial innovation as an example (and, concomitantly, the differences in attitude toward government support of demonstration and commercialization programs). To the Reagan administration, the issue of direct government intervention to foster innovation or even to support commercial demonstration projects assumed symbolic significance that transcended individual decisions regarding the projects themselves. It provided the central focus of a major change that the administration was trying to bring about in all the relations of the federal government with the private sector. Frederick Khedouri, OMB associate director for natural resources, energy, and science, con-

62. Interview by author with William O. Baker, September 30, 1981.

63. Office of Management and Budget, *Additional Details on Budget Savings* (Washington, D.C., April 1981), p. 66; *AAAS Report, 1982* (Washington, D.C.: American Association for the Advancement of Science, 1982), pp. 92–95.

trasted the Reagan administration's approach with that of the Carter administration this way:

> What was happening under Carter was what I would call a kind of creeping planned economy, where under the guise of "reindustrialization" and "overriding national needs" the federal government was intervening further and further upstream with product development and commercialization. Though defended as filling supposed "voids" in the market, it was really anticompetitive, replete with bureaucratic and political prejudices and the desire to manipulate the outcome of the struggles of competing technologies in a capitalist economy.[64]

Schleede took direct issue with the defense by President Carter's science adviser, Frank Press, of the CARP program for joint public-private collaboration on basic automotive research:

> There is not a single project that was talked about under CARP (combustion, corrosion, or aerodynamics research, for instance) that could not and should not be done by the automobile manufacturers themselves—and they *will* do it at any time they really think they need it and there's a payoff down the road.[65]

64. Khedouri interview.
65. Schleede interview.

4

The Fiscal 1982 and 1983 Research and Development Budgets

In March 1981, the Reagan administration's proposed budget for the conduct of all federal R & D programs was $35.5 billion in fiscal 1981 and $40.8 billion in fiscal 1982. This compared with a request by the outgoing Carter administration for $35.5 billion in fiscal 1981 and $41.5 billion in fiscal 1982. The revised Reagan budget in March provided for a 15 percent R & D increase between 1981 and 1982, compared with an 18 percent increase in the original Carter budgets (table 1).[1]

The most important Reagan changes were an increased emphasis on defense R & D and a comcomitant deemphasis on R & D programs in all other functional areas. For fiscal 1981, the Reagan administration made supplementary requests for increases of almost $600 million for defense R & D and rescissions of almost $400 million in all other areas. The proposed changes in the fiscal 1982 budget authority added about $1.5 billion for defense R & D and subtracted about $2.2 billion from all other areas combined.[2] Reviewing the past two years and comparing the 1980 R & D budget with the revised fiscal 1982 Reagan budget, one can see significant shifts regarding not only defense but other areas as well. Defense R & D between fiscal 1980 and fiscal 1982 rose from 47 percent of total federal R & D dollars to 57 percent. In the same period, space declined from 15 percent to 14 percent, health from 12 percent to 10 percent, and energy from 11 percent to 7 percent. In 1982, the four leading R & D support areas—defense, space, health, and energy—accounted for 88 percent of the total. General science accounted for 4 percent, natural resources and

1. National Science Foundation (NSF), *Federal R & D Funding, Fiscal Years 1980–1982*, pp. 1–3.
2. Ibid., p. 1

TABLE 1

BUDGET AUTHORITY FOR RESEARCH AND DEVELOPMENT, BY BUDGET FUNCTION, 1980–1982

(millions of dollars)

	1980	1981			1982		
	Actual	January estimate	Proposed change	Revised March estimate	January estimate	Proposed change	Revised March estimate
National defense	14,946	17,845	597	18,442	21,781	1,481	23,261
Space research and technology	4,587	4,938	−9	4,929	6,048	−509	5,539
Health	3,694	3,850	−25	3,825	4,151	−109	4,043
Energy	3,603	3,679	−164	3,515	3,700	−684	3,016
General science	1,233	1,378	−74	1,304	1,596	−155	1,441
Natural resources and environment	999	1,054	−16	1,038	1,125	−149	976
Transportation	887	897	−19	877	1,033	−150	883
Agriculture	585	653	−6	647	727	−2	725

Education, training, employment, and social services	468	368	−30	339	572	−273	299
Veterans benefits and services	126	140	−2	138	155	−10	146
International affairs	125	125	−2	124	236	−97	138
Commerce and housing credit	101	114	−4	110	127	−6	121
Community and regional development	119	139	−18	121	153	−62	91
Income security	47	62	−1	62	63	−8	55
Administration of justice	45	29	−2	28	46	−15	31
General government	22	27	−1	26	28	−5	23
Total	31,588	35,299	+224	35,523	41,541	−752	40,789

NOTES: The data are listed in descending order of 1982 revised R & D budget authority. One budget function—general science, space, and technology—has been divided into two functions in this analysis: space research and technology, and general science. Detail may not add to totals because of rounding.
SOURCE: National Science Foundation.

environment, transportation, and agriculture for 2 percent each. The remaining functions together made up 2 percent.[3] In September 1981, the administration submitted new budget reduction proposals, which lowered the total R & D budget authority to $38 billion; $22.3 billion went for defense R & D programs and $15.6 billion for nondefense R & D programs.

Basic Research

The Reagan administration continued, throughout the 1981 congressional budget debates and the behind-the-scenes discussions of the fiscal 1983 budget, to voice strong support for basic research. At a gathering of some of the nation's top scientists at the National Academy of Sciences in November 1981, Frederick Khedouri, associate director of the Office of Management and Budget (OMB), said that in comparison with the budget cuts proposed in other areas, "basic research activities" were "absolutely flourishing," and he affirmed the administration's intention to support "some real growth in the aggregate" of basic research to the "extent . . . possible," given the overall budget constraints. Khedouri added, however, that just because the Reagan administration placed a high value on basic research it did not follow that "every penny that we found in the Carter budget for 1982" for new or ongoing research projects "is intrinsically of great merit simply because it bears the label of basic research." At the same gathering, Reagan's science adviser, George Keyworth, continuing his theme that difficult choices would have to be made, accused the scientific community of a "continuing tolerance of mediocrity" and said that some areas of basic research could count on increases but others would face decreases. Both officials rejected any notion that basic research should automatically receive real spending increases each year.[4]

Basic Research Budgets for 1981, 1982. The Carter administration left proposals for basic research funding at $5.1 billion in fiscal 1981 and $5.9 billion in fiscal 1982. The Reagan administration's March 1981 revisions reduced these to $5.0 billion and $5.5 billion, respectively. The further 12 percent reductions proposed by President Reagan in September 1981 brought the basic research budget for fiscal 1982

3. Ibid., p. 2.

4. Frederick Khedouri and George A. Keyworth, statements to the Conference on Federal Research and Development for 1982 and Future Years, National Academy of Sciences, Washington, D.C., October 26, 1981; see also "Academy Parley Bewails the Budget Crunch," *Science and Government Report*, November 1, 1981, pp. 1–4.

down to $5.0 billion. According to data compiled by Willis H. Shapley of the American Association for the Advancement of Science (AAAS), the final Reagan budget cuts resulted in a real decrease of 11 percent for basic research from fiscal 1980 through fiscal 1982 (table 2).[5]

In regard to individual agencies, figures compiled by the AAAS show that the largest two-year increase (1980–1982) resulting from the initial Reagan budget was in the Department of Defense (DOD; 31.2 percent in current dollars; 11.9 percent in constant dollars). The next largest increase was in the Department of Energy (20.0 percent in current dollars; 10.9 percent in constant dollars). Two other major patrons of basic research, the National Science Foundation (NSF) and the National Institutes of Health (NIH), lagged far behind: NSF plus 14.5 percent in current dollars, minus 2.4 percent in constant dollars; and NIH plus 14.6 percent in current dollars, minus 2.3 percent in constant dollars.[6] In total dollars, the agency ranking for basic research as a result of the revised Reagan fiscal 1982 budget was as follows: Health and Human Services Department ($2 billion); NSF ($950 million); DOD ($724 million); DOE ($680 million); National Aeronautics and Space Administration (NASA) ($592 million); and Agriculture Department ($391 million).[7]

Priorities. The Reagan administration made it clear from the outset that the so-called hard sciences—physical and biological sciences— would receive higher priority than the soft, or social and behavioral, sciences.

There is no published compilation of the budget numbers broken down by basic scientific disciplines. A review, however, of the hard science and engineering elements of the NSF, DOD, NASA, NIH, and DOE budgets (including, among others, physics, chemistry, materials research, astronomy, oceanography, mathematics and computers, atmospheric sciences, and the basic engineering programs: electrical, civil, chemical, and mechanical engineering) reveals that in general they held their own. There were a few increases, and cuts were below the average for the rest of the budget. (See tables 3 and 4 for NSF and DOD basic research budgets.)[8]

5. Willis H. Shapley, statement and fact sheet submitted to the Conference on Federal Research and Development for 1982 and Future Years, National Academy of Sciences, Washington, D.C., October 26, 1981. The fact sheet is printed in "Academy Parley Bewails the Budget Crunch," p. 3.

6. *AAAS Report, 1982* (Washington, D.C.: American Association for the Advancement of Science, 1982), pp. 22–24.

7. Ibid., p. 23.

8. NSF, *Federal R & D Funding*, pp. 6–8, 14–15, 22–27, 38, 46–60; and *AAAS Report, 1982*, pp. 20–24, 34–46, 124, 128, 132, 136–38, 144–46.

TABLE 2

ESTIMATED TOTAL FUNDS FOR BASIC RESEARCH, 1980–1982
(millions of dollars)

Agency	Actual FY 1980	March Budget FY 1981	March Budget FY 1982	September Amended Budget FY 1982	September Amended Budget Change from March budget	September Amended Budget % Change from FY 1980
DOD	552	617	724	724	0	+ 31.2
Other	4,164	4,396	4,818	4,240	−578	+ 1.8
Total	4,716	5,013	5,542	4,964	−578	+ 5.3

NOTE: The budget authority includes R & D facilities.
SOURCE: American Association for the Advancement of Science.

TABLE 3

REAGAN AND CARTER BUDGETS FOR R & D IN THE NATIONAL SCIENCE
FOUNDATION, 1981–1982
(millions of dollars)

Scientific Discipline	FY 1981		FY 1982	
	Carter	Reagan	Carter	Reagan
Mathematical and physical sciences	257.1	248.2	301.3	295.4
Mathematical sciences	28.2	27.2	34.4	33.7
Computer research	22.4	21.6	27.5	27.0
Physics	72.2	69.7	83.6	82.0
Chemistry	57.8	55.9	67.2	65.9
Materials research	76.5	73.9	88.6	86.8
Engineering	86.8	83.8	104.6	102.6
Electrical, computer, and systems engineering	23.5	22.6	29.1	28.4
Chemical and process engineering	18.1	17.5	22.1	21.7
Civil and environmental engineering	28.6	27.6	32.6	32.0
Mechanical engineering and applied mechanics	16.6	16.1	20.8	20.4
Biological, behavioral, and social sciences	198.1	183.1	219.0	172.0
Physiology, cellular and molecular biology	77.7	77.7	84.3	82.7
Behavioral and neural sciences	39.6	34.6	43.6	29.2
Social and economic sciences	33.6	23.6	40.1	10.1
Environmental biology	41.1	41.1	44.7	43.9
Information science and technology	6.1	6.1	6.3	6.2
Astronomical, atmospheric, earth, and ocean sciences	236.2	228.0	268.0	253.1
Astronomical sciences	58.5	56.5	75.6	63.8
Atmospheric sciences	68.9	66.5	74.4	73.2
Earth sciences	27.9	26.9	30.6	30.1
Ocean sciences	75.0	72.4	81.0	79.7
Arctic research	5.9	5.7	6.4	6.3

(Table continues)

69

TABLE 3 (continued)

Scientific Discipline	FY 1981		FY 1982	
	Carter	Reagan	Carter	Reagan
Ocean drilling programs	22.0	22.0	30.0	26.0
Antarctic program	64.7	64.7	70.1	70.1
Scientific, technological, and international affairs	56.4	36.0	80.0	37.7
Industrial S&T innovation	25.9	16.9	45.8	17.2
Intergovernmental and public service S&T	8.9	1.5	9.4	1.7
International cooperative scientific activities	14.1	10.1	16.6	10.6
All others	7.5	7.5	8.2	8.2
Cross-directorate programs	26.8	16.2	97.9	—
Research facilities and instrumentation	8.1	6.1	80.7	—
Research initiation and improvement	16.9	8.3	13.0	—
Honorary awards	0.2	0.2	0.2	—
Planning and evaluation	1.6	1.6	4.0	—
Program development and management	61.7	60.7	67.2	63.2
Science education development and research	15.1	8.1	16.2	—
Special foreign currency appropriation (research)	4.5	4.5	2.5	2.5
Total	1,029.4	955.3	1,256.8	1,022.6

NOTES: Science education other than R & D is excluded. Detail may not add to totals because of rounding.
SOURCE: American Association for the Advancement of Science.

In explaining the reasoning behind the Reagan administration's decision to cut back funding for the social and behavioral sciences,

TABLE 4

DEPARTMENT OF DEFENSE FUNDING FOR BASIC RESEARCH,
BY DISCIPLINE, 1981–1982
(millions of dollars)

Scientific Discipline	FY 1981 Est.	FY 1982 Budget
Physics, radiation sciences, astronomy, astrophysics	76.4	88.3
Mechanics and energy conversion	63.1	77.4
Materials	54.1	63.1
Electronics	59.3	75.6
Oceanography	43.6	51.1
Biological and medical sciences	52.3	64.8
Chemistry	48.2	57.7
Mathematics and computer sciences	44.6	53.6
Atmospheric sciences	22.8	26.7
Terrestrial sciences	21.1	25.2
Behavioral and social sciences	18.8	22.8
Aeronautical sciences	10.8	12.9
Subtotal	515.1	619.2
Defense Advanced Research Projects Agency	97.7	95.0
Uniformed Services University of the Health Sciences	1.4	1.6
Total	614.2	715.8

SOURCE: American Association for the Advancement of Science.

OMB executive associate director Glenn Schleede said:

> Though the judgment may seem a harsh one, we just couldn't see that much of the work supported in these areas would contribute to our major goals of enhancing technological innovation and increasing economic growth. With the really tight budget situation, it seemed more important to protect basic research in the physical and biological sciences.[9]

9. Interview with Glenn R. Schleede, executive associate director, OMB, September 9, 1981.

71

Although Schleede denied there were any ideological reasons for the social science cuts, OMB Director David Stockman had in the past associated the "pet theories" of "econometricians, educationists, and social science 'fixers'" with the faults of the Great Society. In an alternative budget document he prepared in 1980 while a congressman, Stockman said:

> Research in the social sciences, education, and economics may produce long-run improvements in social program design and operation [but] there is a strong case to be made that overreliance on the pet theories of the econometricians, educationists, and social science "fixers" has *created* the vast gulf between federal spending and resultant social benefit that we now seek desperately to close. Given present fiscal realities, such research is a very low priority, and funding should be cut back drastically in the short term.[10]

The fiscal 1982 Reagan budget for the social sciences sharply reflected these revised priorities. The NSF Division of Social and Economic Sciences was dropped from the $40.1 million requested by President Carter to $10.1 million. The NSF Behavioral and Neural Science Division was dropped from the $43.6 million requested by Carter to $29.2 million.[11]

Another major source of support for social science research is the Alcohol, Drug Abuse, and Mental Health Administration (ADAMHA) in the Department of Health and Human Services. After the Reagan administration took office, ADAMHA announced that at the end of fiscal 1981 it would end all support for social science research and shift its priorities to biomedical research. In the Department of Education, the National Institute of Education was scheduled for a reduction to $61.0 million, which was almost 10 percent below its fiscal 1981 budget.[12]

In addition to the deep cuts in social science R & D programs, there were two program reductions in the NSF budget that were painful to the academic science community. The first was the decision by OMB to eliminate a Carter administration initiative of $75 million to upgrade aging scientific equipment in university laboratories. The

10. Philip J. Hilts, "White House Uses Social Sciences, but Cuts Funding for Research," *Washington Post*, June 29, 1981. For other reactions to the cuts in social science research, see Constance Holden, "Dark Days for Social Research," *Science*, March 27, 1981, pp. 1397–98; idem, "Science Education Axed," *Science*, March 20, 1981, p. 1330; "Social Science Cuts: Proxmire Triumphant," *Science and Government Report*, April 1, 1981, pp. 1–3; and Frederick Mosteller, "Taking Science Out of Social Science," *Science*, April 17, 1981, p. 102.

11. Holden, "Dark Days," pp. 1397–98; *AAAS Report, 1982*, pp. 11–12, 34–36, 69–72.

12. *AAAS Report, 1982*, pp. 11–12, 34–36, 69–72.

second was a drastic reduction—and virtual elimination—of NSF's graduate fellowship program in science and engineering (Carter fiscal 1982 budget, $81 million; Reagan fiscal 1982 budget, $10 million). In an interview, NSF Director John B. Slaughter (a holdover from the Carter administration) said of the cuts:

> I personally do not think they symbolize a generally negative attitude within the administration toward basic or academic research. The graduate education programs, I think we at the NSF would have to admit, had drifted for several years and were in disarray. I think this blow will allow us to regroup and put together more effective proposals that will pass OMB scrutiny.

He said the elimination of the program to upgrade university laboratory equipment was

> a mistake. . . . It was an example of one of those mishaps that occur with changes of administrations. This is a problem that was first identified during the Ford administration, and I think that with better communication we can turn the OMB around on this one. Jay Keyworth has been very supportive since he arrived.

(Keyworth expressed support for the program in a number of forums during 1981.)[13]

Space

Two important facts emerged from the evolution of space policy during the first year of the Reagan administration. First, the administration, like others since that of President Nixon, assigned top priority to completing the space shuttle transportation system. Ignoring the advice of conservative, free-market institutions like the Heritage Foundation, it did not immediately institute a major reexamination of the costs and benefits of the shuttle versus expendable rockets. Second, the administration's budget reductions for space, coming after a decade of increasing constriction of the space budget, forced a major reevaluation of the total space agency program. NASA officials told the White House that they no longer could balance and adjust the four major program areas—space shuttle, aeronautics research, space science (including planetary exploration), and space applications— and that it should consider dropping one entire program area.

NASA Administrator James M. Beggs said at the end of 1981: "A

13. Ibid.; interview with John B. Slaughter, director, NSF, August 18, 1981.

lot of chickens have come home to roost."[14] He stated that when the decision was made in the early 1970s to go forward with the shuttle, there was an "understanding" with OMB that NASA's total budget would be maintained at about $3.4 billion in constant 1972 dollars. Had this agreement been kept, Beggs said, the NASA budget in the early 1980s would be $7.5–8.0 billion instead of its current $6 billion. The decade-long erosion, he said, had finally produced the need for a major review of the U.S. space effort and perhaps for a jettisoning of whole program areas:

> We have told the White House that it no longer makes sense—from an economic point of view or from the likely scientific payoff—to continue to attempt to squeeze down and juggle all four of the major program areas. They should face up to the possibility of scrapping an entire space activity, such as space science or applications, completely.

Such a decision, he said, would have to be made at the presidential level, and it would hinge upon the administration's funding level for space for fiscal years 1983 and 1984.

Reagan Space Budgets for 1981, 1982. The Carter administration had proposed a sizable increase in the NASA budget for fiscal 1982, from $5.5 billion in fiscal 1981 to $6.7 billion in fiscal 1982 (including construction of facilities). The incoming Reagan administration made a slight reduction in March in the fiscal 1981 figures, but made a large reduction in the proposed 1982 space budget, dropping the total from $6.7 billion to $6.1 billion. NASA, however, was one of the few federal agencies to escape the full budget reduction proposed by the administration in September 1981. Rather than having to absorb the 12 percent cuts decreed for other agencies, NASA was docked only 6 percent. Thus the final administration proposal for the space agency in fiscal 1982 was $5.8 billion. (See table 5 for breakdown of NASA budget categories.)[15]

In explaining the reductions from the Carter space budget proposals for fiscal 1982, Reagan administration budget documents affirmed that federal support for space technology was "an important investment in the nation's future." But they went on to say that the "sharp increase [21 percent] proposed for the space programs in NASA in the [Carter] budget is incompatible with a program of

---

14. Interview with James M. Beggs, NASA administrator, September 11, 1981.
15. *AAAS Report, 1982*, pp. 133–35; see also NSF, *Federal R & D Funding*, pp. 9–10.

TABLE 5

REAGAN AND CARTER BUDGETS FOR NATIONAL AERONAUTICS
AND SPACE ADMINISTRATION, 1981–1982
(millions of dollars)

	FY 1981 Carter	FY 1981 Reagan	FY 1982 Carter	FY 1982 Reagan
Research and development				
Space transportation systems	2,681.1	2,733.6	3,304.2	3,136.1
Space shuttle	1,943.0	2,003.0	2,230.0	2,194.0
Space flight operations	683.7	676.2	1,043.0	910.9
Expendable launch vehicles	54.4	54.4	31.2	31.2
Space science	562.5	538.5	756.7	584.2
Physics and astronomy	344.7	320.7	451.4	325.4
Planetary exploration	175.6	175.6	256.1	215.3
Life sciences	42.2	42.2	49.2	43.5
Space and terrestrial applications	365.4	338.4	487.5	377.5
Space applications	353.6	331.6	472.9	372.9
Technology utilization	11.8	6.8	14.6	4.6
Aeronautics and space technology	390.8	384.8	469.0	390.1
Aeronautical research and technology	276.2	272.2	323.6	264.8
Space research and technology	110.7	110.7	141.0	125.3
Energy technology	3.9	1.9	4.4	—
Space tracking and data acquisition	341.1	341.1	435.2	415.2
Total, research and development	4,340.8	4,336.3	5,452.6	4,903.1
Construction of facilities	115.0	115.0	136.8	104.8
Research and program development	1,081.4	1,071.4	1,136.3	1,114.3
Total, budget plan	5,537.2	5,522.7	6,725.7	6,122.2

NOTE: Detail may not add to totals because of rounding.
SOURCE: American Association for the Advancement of Science.

overall restraint."[16] Because of the revised 1982 budget, NASA eliminated or deferred all new program initiatives and stretched out a number of ongoing projects.

Space shuttle. The one program considered inviolate was the space shuttle. Because the space shuttle currently makes up about 55 percent of the space agency's budget, other program areas were squeezed disproportionately.

The Reagan administration proposed that funding for the space shuttle and for space flight operations be increased, from $2.7 billion in fiscal 1981 to $3.1 billion in fiscal 1982. These levels preserved two initial flights in 1981 and an operational fleet of four orbiters for civilian and military needs by 1984. The option for a fifth orbiter was retained.[17]

The space shuttle in 1981 ran almost 30 percent above its original 1972 cost estimates and was three years behind schedule. Because of the delays, the initial operating schedule of civilian and defense missions through 1985 had been drastically cut, from forty-eight to thirty-two, with another eight missions depending on current budget negotiations. Further, NASA found that operating costs for maintaining and refurbishing the reusable parts of the system were greater than expected and that the turnaround time between missions was going to be longer than originally projected.[18]

The technical difficulties and cost overruns that have plagued shuttle development have raised questions about the wisdom of the program. At the outset of the administration, the Heritage Foundation, which had some influence on the administration, directly challenged the economic justifications offered for the shuttle. It compared the economics of the shuttle and of expendable rockets:

> Gross shuttle costs are now on the order of $3 billion per year. Resumed production of [expendable rockets] would cost several hundred million dollars per year, with a new unmanned expendable development adding no more than a few hundreds of million to this annual figure. Consequently, the early net savings from terminating the shuttle program

16. Executive Office of the President, *A Program for Economic Recovery* (Washington, D.C., February 18, 1981), pp. 6–35; see also John Noble Wilford, "Space Agency Sees Time of Sacrifice," *New York Times*, September 20, 1981; idem, "At NASA, All That's Up Is the Shuttle Columbia," *New York Times*, November 1, 1981.

17. NSF, *Federal R & D Funding*, pp. 11–13; *AAAS Report, 1982*, pp. 59, 133–35.

18. Wilford, "At NASA, All That's Up"; National Aeronautics and Space Administration, "Space Shuttle Program Costs," *NASA Fact Sheet* (April 1981).

are approximately $2 billion, more than one-quarter of the space and general science budget.[19]

The report concluded:

In spite of the received wisdom that there is no turning back on the shuttle commitment, the alternatives should be reviewed thoroughly and soon. Alternatives to be examined should include a discontinuation of the shuttle program, a variable mix of shuttle and expendable launch vehicles, and the possible development of a new expendable vehicle.[20]

Beggs said that the administration had been "aware of" the foundation's recommendation, but that "there was no disposition so far as I know to follow that advice." He added: "These issues were all argued over a decade ago. We think that, despite some of the interim difficulties, the shuttle will ultimately pay its way; and it gives us capabilities far beyond those attainable with expendable vehicles."[21]

Space science. The Reagan administration proposed $538 million for space science in fiscal 1981 and $584 million in fiscal 1982 (the Carter recommendations were $563 million and $757 million, respectively). The reduced funding allowed two important space science projects to proceed more or less on schedule: the space telescope and the Jupiter planetary mission, which is scheduled for a 1985 launch by the space shuttle.

Funding for two other space science projects—the Venus Orbiting Imaging Radar (VOIR) and the Gamma Ray Observatory (GRO)—was substantially reduced in fiscal 1982, and their launch dates were delayed. Both will be launched in 1988, instead of 1986 as originally planned. Finally, the most important U.S. contribution to the International Solar Polar Mission—a U.S. spacecraft—was eliminated, leaving U.S. participation in the project diminished.[22]

Space applications. The Reagan administration proposed $338 million for space applications in fiscal 1981 and $378 million in fiscal 1982 (the Carter recommendations were $365 million and $488 million, respectively). The reduction from the Carter fiscal 1982 budget of $110

19. Eugene J. McAllister, ed., *Agenda for Progress* (Washington, D.C.: Heritage Foundation, 1981), pp. 72–73.

20. Ibid., p. 72.

21. Beggs interview.

22. NSF, *Federal R & D Funding,* pp. 14–15; *AAAS Report, 1982,* p. 135; see also M. Mitchell Waldrop, "Space Science in the Year of the Shuttle," *Science,* April 17, 1981; and idem, "Planetary Science *in extremis,"* *Science,* December 18, 1981.

million from space applications caused a number of cancellations and deferrals, but it allowed continued development on schedule of the LANDSAT-D earth resources survey satellite and a number of other smaller atmospheric and geological survey experiments. Several interagency projects proposed by the Carter administration in fiscal 1981 were either curtailed drastically or canceled. Among them were the National Oceanic Satellite System (NOSS) to provide global ocean data (eliminated); the AGRISTARS program for agricultural and natural resources survey (significantly reduced); and the Geological Applications Program (GAP) to improve global surveys of mineral and energy resources (eliminated). Finally, in keeping with overall administration policy regarding the proper role of the federal government, the space applications technology transfer program was eliminated and a technology utilization program substantially cut back.[23]

Aeronautics. NASA's aeronautics research program was singled out by the Heritage Foundation as an illustration of the use of public funds for commercially applicable research that the private sector could undertake. The foundation called for a review of such programs and urged the federal government to back out of them entirely. The report stated that the

> criterion for such a federal backout should be that the benefits of an innovation are sufficiently appropriable to the firm developing it (through patents, trade secrets, copyrights, or even entrance into the market) that the private sector has enough incentives to decide whether to invest in the innovation. . . . A particular area in which application of this concern should result in substantial federal backout is NASA's program for aeronautical research and technology.[24]

The Reagan administration partially followed the advice of the foundation report in the initial fiscal 1982 budget. The budget totals for aeronautical research did not decline drastically—as would have occurred if the report's recommendations had been fully implemented—but the criteria for the reductions followed the broad outlines of the report. The administration stated that the "revised budget preserves the fundamental research activities having broad civil and military applicability," and that reductions were "focused on ongoing technology development and demonstration activities which are more appropriately the responsibility of the private sector."[25]

23. NSF, *Federal R & D Funding*, pp. 16–17; *AAAS Report, 1982*, pp. 60, 135.

24. McAllister, *Agenda for Progress*, p. 75.

25. Office of Management and Budget (OMB), *Additional Details on Budget Savings* (Washington, D.C., April 1981), p. 302.

The Carter administration had proposed $276 million in fiscal 1981 and $324 million in fiscal 1982 for aeronautics research and demonstration; the Reagan revisions decreased these totals to $272 million in fiscal 1981 and $265 million in fiscal 1982. Among the programs cut back or eliminated on the basis of the administration's criteria were the Numerical Aerodynamic Simulator, a computer system to produce simulations of advanced aircraft aerodynamic designs (indefinitely deferred); activities to produce more energy-efficient jet engines (cut back); V/STOL systems technology (deferred); and work on variable cycle engines (deferred).[26]

The Future. The decision of the OMB to hold the line on the NASA budget near the current figure of $6 billion made negotiations difficult during the fall of 1981. NASA officials advanced various options on behalf of their belief that the agency must drastically cut back in large program areas. Beggs said in an interview that his personal recommendation would be to curtail space application projects. Attention instead has focused on the space science area—particularly on large-scale planetary exploration projects, which OMB had publicly warned were becoming too expensive.[27] Keyworth, the president's science adviser, maintained that, within the space science field, orbiting laboratories, like the space telescope or the Gamma Ray Observatory, will result in a larger scientific payoff than additional planetary probes. Keyworth told *Science:* "I just think that the scientific potential of trying to exploit astronomy and astrophysics is much greater than would be achieved by continuing to put primary emphasis on the planetary program."[28] During the fiscal 1983 budget negotiations, discussion centered on whether to cancel both the Jupiter mission and the VOIR mission. NASA also established an advisory committee to explore less expensive planetary probers, with the aim of holding costs to $150–200 million rather than the $1 billion of the current missions.

Space shuttle. Finally, NASA Administrator Beggs said in an interview that within the next four or five years the space agency should begin planning to spin off the space shuttle system to the private sector:

> Once the system is fully operational it should be taken over by some kind of public-private entity, possibly using COM-

26. NSF, *Federal R & D Funding,* p. 18; *AAAS Report, 1982,* pp. 60–61, 135.

27. Beggs interview; see also "NASA Chief Balks at New Budget Cut Order," *Science and Government Report,* December 1981, pp. 1–3.

28. Waldrop, "Planetary Science."

SAT as a model. The federal bureaucracy just isn't very good at long-term management of large-scale operations like a space transportation system on a cost-effective basis. One big problem is that because of political interference and the resulting uncertainties you often don't get sound management decisions.

I think that the space shuttle system will be commercially viable and if well-run could give an excellent return on investment.[29]

Beggs's views here parallel the recommendations of the Heritage Foundation, which also argued for ultimately turning over the space transportation system to the private sector:

A longer-term approach would be for the federal government to turn the space transportation business over to the private sector and to purchase space transportation services as necessary for research and national defense activities. Competing firms would develop, produce, and operate launch vehicles, similar to the way that many firms under federal and private contracts now produce and operate space satellites. The launch facilities and the tracking and data acquisition system would be sold or leased to the private sector. . . . investment decisions as to what mix of launch vehicle types to develop and operate would be left up to the private sector.[30]

It is entirely plausible that the civilian applications and scientific missions might be handed over to the private sector, but both Beggs and the Heritage Foundation have probably underestimated the real problems that would ensue in the defense area. It is not likely that the Defense Department—or Congress—would look with favor upon a scheme by which they had to depend on a private or semiprivate company for key military services in space.

Defense

In sharp contrast to the 1976 presidential campaign, the 1980 campaign saw neither candidate claim that reductions in the total defense budget were possible. Indeed, President Carter and Ronald Reagan limited their debate to the adequacy of the significant increases in the defense spending already projected by the Carter administration. Reagan, as a candidate and as president, committed himself to re-

29. Beggs interview.
30. McAllister, *Agenda for Progress*, p. 73.

directing federal spending priorities, with huge increases in defense spending leading the way.

President Reagan's revised fiscal 1981 and 1982 budgets carried out this campaign promise. The original March 1981 Reagan revisions called for a defense expenditure increase from about 25 percent of the total federal budget in fiscal 1981 to about 29 percent in fiscal 1982 (under President Carter's fiscal 1982 budget, defense spending was scheduled for only 25 percent of the federal budget totals).[31]

Defense R & D spending (almost exclusively derived from DOD and Energy Department programs) was originally projected by the Reagan administration to increase from $18.4 billion in fiscal 1981 to $23.3 billion in fiscal 1982 (comparable Carter figures were $17.8 billion in fiscal 1981 and $21.8 billion in fiscal 1982). Of this total, Defense Department R & D would increase under Reagan from $17.1 billion in fiscal 1981 to $21.7 billion in fiscal 1982 (Carter: $16.5 billion in fiscal 1981 and $20.3 billion in fiscal 1982). Under President Reagan's original proposals, defense R & D increased to 57 percent of the total federal R & D budget, up significantly from 47 percent in fiscal 1980. (See table 6 for details on the defense R & D budget.)[32]

Under the September 1981 Reagan administration budget revisions, total defense R & D was reduced from $23.3 billion to $22.3 billion, but because of even more reductions in nondefense R & D spending, defense R & D spending increased under these revisions from 57 percent to almost 60 percent of total federal R & D spending.[33]

Reagan Defense R & D Priorities. The Reagan administration in its first year did not develop a comprehensive defense R & D policy statement comparable to that left behind by William J. Perry, under secretary of defense for research and engineering in the Carter administration. The most detailed review of the new administration's ideas came in testimony in March 1981 before the Senate Defense Appropriations Subcommittee by the acting under secretary of defense for research and engineering, James P. Wade, Jr.[34] Wade's state-

31. NSF, *Federal R & D Funding*, p. 5.

32. Ibid., pp. 5–6.

33. NSF, "Highlights," December 15, 1981, Science Resources Studies.

34. Department of Defense, *The Department of Defense Statement on the Budget and Programs for Research, Development and Acquisition*, statement by Honorable James P. Wade, Jr., acting under secretary of defense for research and engineering and assistant to the secretary of defense for atomic energy, March 11, 1981 (hereafter cited as DOD, *R & D Programs, 1982*). Subsequent quotations from James P. Wade, Jr., are from this statement.

TABLE 6

R & D BUDGET AUTHORITY FOR NATIONAL DEFENSE, 1980–1982
(millions of dollars)

	1980	1981			1982		
	Actual	January estimate	Proposed change	Revised March estimate	January estimate	Proposed change	Revised March estimate
Department of Defense, military	13,813	16,485	597	17,081	20,267	1,479	21,746
Research, development, test, and evaluation	13,345	15,887	597	16,483	19,652	1,479	21,131
Technology base	2,265	2,554	1	2,555	2,949	146	3,095
Advanced technology development	604	603	–3	600	790	–29	761
Strategic programs	2,165	3,470	55	3,525	4,417	535	4,953
Tactical programs	5,233	5,681	481	6,162	6,961	588	7,548
Intelligence and communications	1,152	1,513	37	1,550	1,960	149	2,109
Defense-wide mission support	1,926	2,066	25	2,091	2,575	91	2,666
Other DOD military	468	598	—	598	615	—	615

Atomic energy defense activities						
(Energy Department)	1,133	1,361	—	1,361	1,513	2	1,515
Naval reactor development	241	250	—	250	280	—	280
Weapons research, development, and testing	628	803	—	803	935	20	955
Inertial confinement fusion	113	141	—	141	120	−14	106
Verification and control	11	14	—	14	15	—	15
Materials production	13	18	—	18	33	1	34
Defense nuclear waste management	83	92	—	92	86	−5	81
Nuclear materials and safeguards development	43	43	—	43	44	—	44
Total	14,946	17,845	597	18,442	21,781	1,481	23,261

NOTES: Dashes indicate no change. Detail may not add to totals because of rounding.
SOURCE: National Science Foundation.

ment followed many of the lines already set down by Perry, with greater urgency because the new administration believed that the U.S. position in relation to the Soviet Union had deteriorated over the past decade. Wade said:

> The [30 percent real increase in the DOD R & D budget] reflects the real dangers to U.S. interests throughout the world, the deterioration in our defense posture, and the need to restore quickly and visibly America's defenses as soon as possible. The problem we face is how to rapidly make the moves necessary to redress and reverse the adverse trends in the relative balance in equipment and technology between the U.S. and the Soviet Union.

Wade compared Soviet defense research investment with that of the United States:

> Dollar cost estimates for Soviet military RDT & E [research, development, testing, and evaluation] expenditures have exceeded U.S. expenditures during each of the past 10 years, leading to an aggregate gap of about $90 billion (in 1982 dollars). Their military RDT & E program is now about twice that of the U.S. program. A clear indication of their commitment to defense technology is the trend toward increasing the share of Soviet military outlays devoted to RDT & E.

Despite the decade-long imbalance, Wade said, the United States still maintained leadership in most of the basic defense technologies, "but it was losing that lead in some key technologies." This made it imperative for the United States to continue a "program of real growth in the [defense] science and technology base."

The sizable increases scheduled for defense R & D were not for new programs or priorities. Rather they allowed the DOD to accelerate some existing projects, to start others that had been deferred by the Carter administration, and to support some programs not given priority by the Carter administration.

The acting deputy under secretary for research and advanced technology, George P. Millburn, stated in an interview that the major thrusts outlined in the Perry valedictory were still valid. Thus the Reagan administration, like the Carter administration, placed major defense R & D emphasis on the modernization of U.S. strategic forces; on improved antiarmor capability; on the maintenance of air and naval superiority; on the improvement of rapid deployment capabilities; and on the upgrading of the defense technology base. Millburn projected major changes in the management of defense R & D. The Reagan administration, he said, would place a much higher emphasis on getting technology "out of the laboratory, off the shelf, and into use." Millburn added:

> There is always a tendency for the researchers to want to stay on the cutting edge of research to fine-tune a technology just a little bit more. This can be extremely costly and time consuming. I think you'll see a major effort to speed up the R & D process and to get hardware and systems into use, into the field.[35]

Among the priority areas inherited from the Carter administration, Millburn said the Reagan administration would continue to stress modernizing strategic forces. He cited the decision of the new administration—reversing an action of President Carter—to proceed with a new strategic bomber (B-1 to replace the B-52). He also cited the decision to begin developing a new submarine-based missile (Trident II to replace the Trident I).

Technology base. Another area of particuar concern and priority—as it had been under both the Ford and the Carter administrations—is the technology base sector of the DOD R & D budget. This consists of basic research, advanced exploratory development, and advanced technology development categories. Within this area are encompassed the long-term basic and applied research projects that underpin the military technology of the future. Both the Carter and the Reagan fiscal 1981 and fiscal 1982 budgets provided substantial real increases for the technology base (from $3.2 billion in fiscal 1981 to $3.9 billion in fiscal 1982).[36]

Basic Research. The March 1981 Reagan budget recommendation of $724 million for DOD basic research programs contained a real increase of about 8 percent over fiscal 1981. This increase, coming after sizable real increases in 1980 and 1981, signaled that the Reagan administration would support the reemergence of the DOD as a major patron of basic research in many fields (NSF still leads overall, but its budget is not growing as fast as the DOD budget). Defense Secretary Caspar W. Weinberger approved the resurgence of DOD basic research in September 1981, stating that the "national base of basic research is inadequate to meet future DOD needs and substantial sustained real growth in defense research is needed to restore this base."[37]

35. Interview by the author with George P. Millburn, acting DOD deputy under secretary for research and advanced technology, August 18, 1981.

36. NSF, *Federal R & D Funding*, p. 6.

37. Kim A. McDonald, "Defense: A Booming Bankroll for Basic Research," *Science*

Almost all DOD basic research disciplines were designated to receive increased funding in fiscal 1982. The largest increase went to oceanography, followed by research on new materials, biological and medical sciences, mechanics, energy conversion, atmospheric sciences, chemistry, and mathematics. Among the projects targeted for special emphasis, according to Pentagon officials, were:

- free-electron laser research to produce lasers from millimeter to X-ray wavelength
- research on computer software, robotics, and artificial intelligence
- research on human tolerances to environmental extremes, chemical and biological warfare, and low-level radiation
- research on new materials with unusual electrical, optical, and magnetic properties
- physical oceanography[38]

The increases in DOD basic research funds have helped to re-establish Pentagon ties with universities and colleges. More than $300 million of the $724 million for DOD fiscal 1982 basic research is expected to go to universities. This is a 17.4 percent increase over fiscal 1981. The Defense Department also persuaded Congress to simplify the rules governing research. Rather than complex contracts, which were always more appropriate for multibillion-dollar procurements of hardware, the department was granted authority to award simple grants to universities, the details of which could be covered on a one-page form. DOD also requested that the OMB modify the much-disliked Circular A-21, to reduce the burden on university researchers in accounting for the time spent on federally supported research.[39]

Finally, the Defense Department increased its support in fiscal 1982 in two areas scheduled for major cuts in other agencies: social science research and graduate science education. Social science research, though not a large part of the DOD basic research budget, received a small increase in fiscal 1982. DOD, in addition to increasing ROTC fellowships in 1982 (many of which go to students in science and engineering), established a new fellowship program for predoctoral graduate students in science and engineering. By 1984, the

and Government Report, September 15, 1981, pp. 5–6; NSF, Federal R & D Funding, p. 6, and AAAS Report, 1982, p. 54, give slightly different figures for the real increase in DOD basic research spending.

38. McDonald, "Defense: A Booming Bankroll," p. 6; AAAS Report, 1982, p. 124.

39. McDonald, "Defense: A Booming Bankroll," p. 5; AAAS Report, 1982, p. 26.

department plans to support up to 400 such fellowships, with stipends between $10,000 and $12,000 per year.[40]

Millburn, noting the severe shortages of trained graduate students and faculty in engineering, defended the new DOD graduate education programs:

> This is not simply altruism on DOD's part. As we have looked down the road, it has become clear that unless we do something to beef up graduate education in engineering and computer and information sciences, for instance, we are not going to have the trained manpower to retain the technological superiority that is the central element of our advantage over the Soviets. In a sense, these programs are the human resources part of our strategic modernization effort.[41]

Energy

Administration science policy spokesmen invariably cited energy R & D as illustrating one of the sharpest differences in approach and priorities with the Carter administration. "In energy R & D," Keyworth said, "this administration has taken a 180-degree turn." Schleede said that "in energy, we almost completely redefined the federal government's role."[42]

The most comprehensive exposition of the Reagan administration's energy policies, including energy R & D, came in *The National Energy Policy Plan* (NEP), a congressionally mandated administration statement published in July 1981. The NEP directly tied the administration's energy policy to its economic goals and its political philosophy regarding the respective roles of the government and the private sector:

> The administration's reformulation of policies affecting energy is part of the president's comprehensive program for economic recovery, which includes elimination of excessive federal spending and taxes, regulatory relief, and a sound monetary policy. [The aim of the economic recovery program] is to release the strength of the private sector.[43]

40. McDonald, "Defense: A Booming Bankroll," pp. 5–6; Millburn interview.

41. Millburn interview.

42. Interview by the author with George A. Keyworth, director, Office of Science and Technology Policy, September 16, 1981.

43. Department of Energy, *The National Energy Policy Plan*, report to the Congress required by Title VIII of the Department of Energy Organization Act (Public Law 95–91), Washington, D.C., July 1981, p. 3 (hereafter cited as DOE, *National Energy Plan*).

The report went on:

> Public spending for energy-related purposes is secondary to
> ensuring that the private sector can respond to market real-
> ities. . . . The collective judgment of properly motivated in-
> novators, business, and consumers is generally superior to
> any form of centralized programming.

Regarding the government role, the report said:

> Federal spending should be considered only in those prom-
> ising areas of energy production and use where the private
> sector is unlikely to invest. . . . Public spending is appropri-
> ate [and will continue] in long-term research with high risks,
> but potentially high payoffs. In most cases, however, using
> public funds to subsidize either domestic energy production
> or conservation buys little additional security and only di-
> verts capital, workers, and initiative from uses that contrib-
> ute more to society and the economy.[44]

Thus the major purpose of the federal government, under the for-
mulations of the Reagan administration, was to foster private sector
activity—and to intervene rarely and in quite limited ways.

There were two significant shifts in energy policy that had major
effects on R & D policy: an increased emphasis on energy production
over energy conservation; and within the energy production sector, a
tilt toward nuclear energy. These policy revisions, combined with a
determined, if not wholly successful, attempt by the Reagan administration to constrict the role of the government, produced a sea
change in the federal R & D budget.

The proposed withdrawal of administration support for energy
demonstration and development programs was the chief factor in the
significant decreases in energy R & D in fiscal 1982. The Carter administration had proposed $3.7 billion for energy R & D in both fiscal
1981 and 1982. The Reagan administration's initial proposals called for
$3.5 billion in fiscal 1981 and $3.0 billion in fiscal 1982 (the September
1981 proposals reduced this figure to $2.5 billion).[45]

Energy Production Programs

In President Carter's fiscal 1982 budget, nuclear R & D programs
(with R & D plant and equipment figured in) would have made up 41

44. Ibid., pp. 3–4.
45. NSF, *Federal R & D Funding*, pp. 28–29; idem, "Highlights."

percent of the total energy R & D budget and nonnuclear programs 59 percent. The Reagan fiscal 1982 proposals altered these percentages substantially, nuclear programs receiving 72 percent of the total and nonnuclear R & D 28 percent.[46]

Fission. Nuclear fission programs under the Reagan fiscal 1982 budget went up 14 percent; the Carter administration had proposed an 18 percent decrease (Reagan total: $998 million; Carter total: $679 million). The most significant change, in breeder reactor R & D, stemmed from the decision of the administration to restore top priority for the Clinch River breeder reactor demonstration plant. The Reagan 1982 budget almost doubled funds for breeder R & D, requesting $567 million for these programs as compared with the Carter administration's request for $296 million. The Reagan administration also raised the budgets for the commercial nuclear waste programs and for cleanup and research programs relating to the Three Mile Island accident.[47] The Reagan administration continued to provide strong support for long-range fusion research—$311 million in fiscal 1982—though it pared $6 million from the Carter proposal.[48]

Fossil and Synthetic Fuels. On the other side of the energy production R & D ledger were fossil fuels, which dropped dramatically under the Reagan proposals, from $636 million in fiscal 1981 to $411 million in fiscal 1982 (the Carter proposal for fiscal 1981 was $678 million and for fiscal 1982, $754 million). If money for the plant and equipment of proposed synthetic fuels demonstration plants is included, the changes are even more dramatic: the Carter fiscal 1982 proposal was $1.6 billion and the Reagan, $435 million.[49]

The *National Energy Policy Plan* and the documents accompanying the Reagan fiscal 1982 budget detailed the administration's revised strategy for developing fossil and synthetic fuel. In more abbreviated form, this rationale would be repeated in other energy R & D areas, such as solar energy, wind energy, geothermal energy, biomass, urban waste, transportation, and energy storage and transmission programs.

Regarding federal demonstration and commercialization activities in fossil and synthetic fuels, the OMB stated:

46. Calculated from figures provided in *AAAS Report, 1982,* pp. 28–29.
47. NSF, *Federal R & D Funding,* pp. 32–33.
48. Ibid., pp. 34–35.
49. Ibid., pp. 39–40; *AAAS Report, 1982,* pp 28–29.

Costly, near-term activities, such as construction and operation of pilot plants and the operation of demonstration plants using company-specific processes, subsidize industrial companies while producing rapid and uncontrollable growth in the federal budget. The budget in this area has increased dramatically in the last seven years increasing seven-fold primarily because of pressures from private firms to have federal funding spread among many potential private companies.

In 1982, the OMB said, "government outlays are less needed . . . because the energy industry has stepped up its R & D investments (25 percent in 1979 over 1978)," and because Reagan administration policies (deregulation of energy prices, tax incentives, removal of excessive regulatory burdens) "will further enhance the private sector's ability to develop and introduce new technologies." Further, withdrawing federal funds from demonstration and commercialization activities "will make it possible to devote more governmental resources to true research as the more capital-intensive applied and market-oriented federal activities are scaled back."[50]

Synthetic Fuels Commercialization. Despite its rhetoric, the Reagan administration did not move decisively to fulfill its free-market principles in synthetic fuels commercialization. It did not attempt to eliminate either the $17 billion off-budget fund for energy commercialization (largely synthetic fuels) projects that had been set up by Congress or the U.S. Synthetic Fuels Corporation to administer it. When the administration took office, federal support for synthetic fuels demonstration and commercialization consisted of two Department of Energy programs and the projected Synthetic Fuels Corporation. The DOE fossil fuel demonstration program supported five major synthetic fuels projects out of DOE appropriations. In addition, the DOE Alternative Fuels Program had $5.5 billion available in the off-budget energy security reserve fund for interim funding of synthetic fuels demonstrations until the Synthetic Fuels Corporation began operations. Finally, the Synthetic Fuels Corporation was scheduled to have $12.2 billion at its disposal by mid-1982.[51]

The Reagan administration, faced with this somewhat complicated situation, decided to terminate DOE support for the five on-

---

50. OMB, *Additional Details on Budget Savings*, pp. 120–21.

51. For an excellent history of the development of the synthetic fuels program and particularly of the Synthetic Fuels Corporation, see Carrol E. Watts, "The U.S. Synthetic Fuels Program: An Overview," mimeographed (Washington, D.C.: Government Research Corporation, May 4, 1981).

budget demonstration projects, arguing that they could apply later to the Synthetic Fuels Corporation for support from its off-budget reserve fund. During the summer of 1981, however, OMB Director Stockman lost a battle with DOE Secretary James B. Edwards over whether to allow the DOE to commit funds from its off-budget Alternative Fuels Program for three new synthetic fuels demonstration projects. The president sided with Edwards, and the project agreements were signed. When the Synthetic Fuels Corporation officially began operating in October 1981, it planned to make an initial selection from projects that were submitted by more than sixty firms answering the corporation's first solicitation.[52]

Solar Energy. The OMB includes in this category not only solar heating and cooling programs and photovoltaics, but also solar-related technologies, such as wind and ocean systems, alcohol fuels, biomass, and thermal energy systems. The Carter administration had proposed $434 million for these programs in fiscal 1982; the Reagan administration reduced it to $162 million.[53]

The purpose of the reduction, according to OMB documents, was to limit federal support in these areas to "long-term, high-risk [research] with potentially high payoff" and eliminate "nearer term technology development and commercialization activities." This move, stated the OMB, was part of a larger effort "to apply sound economic criteria" in place of the "current subsidy programs." The Reagan administration proposed to leave in place the solar tax credits legislated by Congress, estimating that the credits would reduce taxes for homeowners and businesses by $2.6 billion between 1981 and 1986. Further, it maintained that "deregulation of energy prices [would] provide additional incentive" for increased investment and that other administration policies such as "deregulation of oil and increasing natural gas prices permitted under the Natural Gas Policy Act will remove the subsidies for competing oil and gas technologies that have prevented solar from achieving its true potential." "Under these conditions," stated the OMB, "it is no longer necessary or appropriate for DOE to support costly near-term development, demonstration and commercialization efforts that industry can and will do."[54]

The administration's theory translated into substantial budget reductions for a number of solar-related technologies, including photovoltaics, which was reduced from $160.2 million (fiscal 1981) to

52. Ibid., app. A; Martin Schram, " Reagan Overrides Stockman, Backs Edwards on Synfuels," *Washington Post*, July 30, 1981.

53. NSF, *Federal R & D Funding*, pp. 29–30.

54. OMB, *Additional Details on Budget Savings*, p. 128.

$62.9 million (fiscal 1982) through elimination of the Low-Cost Solar Array commercialization program. Wind energy decreased from $85.8 million (fiscal 1981) to $19.4 million (fiscal 1982), the Ocean Thermal Energy program of $39 million was terminated, the alcohol fuels program was reduced from $27 million (fiscal 1981) to $10 million (fiscal 1982), and the biomass program was cut from $46.5 million (fiscal 1981) to $20.5 million (fiscal 1982).[55]

Other Programs. Two other energy supply programs, geothermal energy and electric and energy storage systems, were also substantially reduced by the Reagan administration. Geothermal energy was reduced to $44 million in fiscal 1982, down from the $67 million proposed by the Carter administration. A hydrothermal industrialization program, which the new administration thought should be left entirely to the private sector, was virtually eliminated.[56] Elimination of development and commercialization activities resulted in reductions of more than half the total cost of electric energy and storage systems, from $96 million in the Carter fiscal 1982 budget to $47 million in the Reagan budget.[57]

Energy Conservation

Energy conservation R & D programs were cut for the same reasons that solar energy programs were: the decontrol of oil and gas prices, combined with existing tax credits, had reduced the necessity for federal intervention. OMB said:

> Motivated by rising energy costs and substantial federal tax credits, individuals, businesses, and other institutions are undertaking major conservation efforts. Evidence of this conservation is clear. In the six years after the Arab oil embargo, total energy consumption increased only 6 percent, compared to an increase of 29 percent in the six years prior to the embargo. With rising energy prices since the oil embargo in 1973, energy consumption per dollar of output has steadily declined every year since, decreasing by a total of 9 percent. Decontrol of oil prices and continuation of tax credits can be expected to accelerate these trends.[58]

Thus, OMB argued, "some federal conservation efforts are no longer needed." The federal government should limit its support to "long-

55. NSF, *Federal R & D Funding,* pp. 29–30; *AAAS Report, 1982,* pp. 29–30.
56. NSF, *Federal R & D Funding,* p. 31.
57. Ibid., p. 36.
58. Executive Office of the President, *A Program for Economic Recovery,* p. 58.

term, generic and high-risk, but potentially high payoff research," it said, and withdraw from "projects where commercial viability can be tested by the private sector alone, including urban waste, consumer products, advanced automotive engine design, demonstration of electric and hybrid vehicles, and industrial processes."[59]

Carrying out these principles, the Reagan administration in March 1981 proposed to reduce the fiscal 1982 energy conservation R & D budget from the $267 million proposed by President Carter to $85 million. The largest reduction came in transportation energy conservation, where the total budget dropped from $115 million to $37 million and forced major cutbacks in vehicle propulsion R & D in the electric and hybrid vehicle R & D programs.[60] Industrial energy conservation R & D was in effect eliminated by a reduction of $50 million, from an existing $51 million program. The building and community systems conservation R & D program was cut to $29 million, from the $69 million proposed by the Carter administration. The remaining funds in building and community systems R & D were to be spent for basic research on the use of energy in buildings and for longer-term research on urban waste.[61]

Critics

In regard to energy R & D strategy and policy, the Reagan administration has found itself criticized by the right, which accuses it of not following its own free-market doctrines, and by the left, which challenges what it considers a double standard applied to nuclear and fossil fuel R & D on the one hand and renewable resources and conservation R & D on the other hand. The left also disagrees with the Reagan administration's ground rules for government intervention into energy development. Two focal points of this debate are the breeder reactor program and the fossil and synthetic fuels program.

Right. Both the breeder reactor program (particularly the Clinch River demonstration plant) and the synthetic fuels subsidy program have been challenged by conservative, free-market-oriented economists and organizations. At the outset of the Reagan administration the Heritage Foundation published *Agenda for Progress*, a primer for government spending cuts calling for a "drastic" reduction in the budget to implement the breeder technology. Of the Clinch River demonstration project, the foundation said: "It is likely that the project is not an effective investment. A cost-benefit analysis would prob-

59. Ibid.
60. NSF, *Federal R & D Funding*, pp. 41–42.
61. Ibid.

ably show that R & D money would be better spent to develop the technology of light water resources."[62]

Several years ago, the American Enterprise Institute published a more detailed critique of the breeder reactor program, *The Liquid Metal Fast Breeder Reactor: An Economic Analysis,* by Brian G. Chow. Chow challenged most of the major assumptions that had produced positive cost-benefit analyses of the breeder—such as the extent of uranium resources, future energy demand, alternative nuclear technologies, plant capital costs for the breeder, and potential cost overruns—and concluded that the breeder technology "yields no net discounted benefits." He recommended that a "portion of the funds for the [breeder programs] be transferred to other [energy] programs" and that the breeder programs be regarded as backups. Chow said:

> Before the nation commits itself more heavily to the [breeder program], it can afford to wait another five to ten years for better projections of future energy demand, better estimates of uranium resources, and a clearer determination of the feasibility of an economically and environmentally acceptable commercial fusion reactor.[63]

One of the most trenchant critiques of the breeder reactor program was delivered by David Stockman, several years before he became the OMB director. In a 1977 "Dear Colleague" letter to Republican congressmen in the House of Representatives opposing continuation of the Clinch River breeder reactor project, he called the vote a "test of whether, as Republicans, we will consistently adhere to the free-market views on energy policy that we so forcefully advocated during the debate on the energy bill earlier this session." He believed in "government support for basic scientific research, laboratory experimentation, and pilot-scale demonstrations," he said, but the "government should not become involved in the provision of subsidies for the commercialization of new energy technologies that cannot pass the market test of competitiveness with alternatives on a price basis." He added that the breeder reactor would not pass this test "until well into the next century, if ever."

Stockman also warned:

> The precedent set by continuing the Clinch River project will be one of increasingly deeper government involvement in the development, marketing, and commercialization of alternative energy sources and massive federal subsidies to un-

62. McAllister, *Agenda for Progress,* p. 94.

63. Brian G. Chow, *The Liquid Metal Fast Breeder Reactor: An Economic Analysis* (Washington, D.C.: American Enterprise Institute, 1975), pp. 71–73.

derwrite future national energy costs. Today it is the nuclear breeder lobby looking for a large, uneconomic subsidy. Tomorrow it will be the solar power gang, then the windmill freaks, and so on in a never-ending stream of outstretched palms.[64]

Two years later, true to this creed, Stockman also took the lead in opposing the creation of a Synthetic Fuels Corporation, which provided for massive subsidies for synthetic fuels development over the next decade. Similarly, the Heritage Foundation, in its 1981 advice to the incoming Reagan administration, argued for the elimination of all subsidies for synthetic fuels and all domestic energy production and conservation programs:

> The budget for promotion of domestic production provides grants and loans at terms more favorable than market terms, or purchase guarantees for solar, biomass, and synthetic fuels. As a general principle, tax dollars are not allocated cost effectively when used to subsidize the direct production of energy. If the output was worth the cost, the private sector would find it profitable to produce the energy without government assistance. . . . There is no justification for supplementing the market to support energy production, and the subsidy to synthetic fuel producers should be eliminated. The same criticism applies to the biomass budget, which provides outlays and loans to convert grain, form residues, and other biomass into synthetic fuels.[65]

Left. Finding common cause on at least one level with conservative critics, environmental and consumer spokesmen in 1981 accused the Reagan administration of employing a double standard in invoking free-market principles. Robert H. Williams of the Princeton University Center for Energy and Environmental Studies, who testified extensively for environmental and consumer groups, calculated that conventional energy supplies, including nuclear and fossil fuels, enjoy federal subsidies of about $6 billion per year. Thus, he said, it was clear that the fate of nuclear power and synthetic fuels was "not being left to the invisible hand of the market."[66]

64. The "Dear Colleague" letter and supporting material are cited in the testimony of Thomas B. Cochran, Natural Resources Defense Council, Inc., before the House Committee on Science and Technology, March 4, 1981.

65. McAllister, *Agenda for Progress*, p. 93.

66. Colin Norman, "Energy Conservation: The Debate Begins," *Science*, April 24, 1981, pp. 424–26; see also testimony of Robert H. Williams, Princeton University Center for Energy and Environmental Studies, "An Energy Conservation Strategy for the 1980s," before the Subcommittee on Energy, Nuclear Proliferation, and Government Processes of the Senate Committee on Governmental Affairs, July 21, 1981; and Eric

Jonathan Lash, president of the Energy Conservation Coalition, a group of environmental and consumer groups formed to lobby for revisions in the Reagan administration's proposed energy budget, stated in an interview:

> It's really hypocritical for administration spokesmen to trot out these "free-market" arguments when they talk about conservation and renewable resource programs and then to support huge increases in subsidies for nuclear power and synthetic fuels. They shouldn't be allowed to have it both ways.[67]

The environmental and consumer coalitions—in addition to citing the administration's own free-market arguments in their attempt to eliminate or reduce federal support of nuclear and synthetic fuels programs—put forward their own positive arguments for increasing federal support for conservation programs.

First, they agree in most instances with reliance on market forces, but they say that for conservation there are gross deficiencies in the marketplace. Williams and others have argued that "the discount rate implicit in many well-documented energy efficiency investment decisions is many times higher than market interest rates, showing vividly that there are major institutional obstacles to well-functioning markets." Williams cites homeowners' energy efficiency investments, building conservation retrofit data, and the experience of consumer purchases of appliances such as air conditioners and refrigerators as examples that show "quantitatively how poorly the markets are working in the area of energy conservation."[68]

Williams's contentions obviously have implications for a number of facets of energy policy, particularly for energy regulatory policy. In regard to federal R & D energy policy, however, Williams and others argue that there are similar market imperfections that will result in underinvestment in conservation R & D by the private sector. In building and other industries, they say, fragmentation and the lack of any tradition of R & D investing operate against an adequate level of R & D investment.[69] They have found some support for this argument

---

Hirst et al., "Improving Energy Efficiency: The Case for Government Action," mimeographed (Energy Division, Oak Ridge National Laboratory, Oak Ridge, Tenn., March 1981).

67. Interview with Jonathan Lash, president, Energy Conservation Coalition, September 16, 1981; see also testimony of Jonathan Lash before the Task Force on Energy and Environment of the House Budget Committee, March 12, 1981.

68. Letter from Robert H. Williams to Senator Mark Hatfield (Republican, Oregon), June 19, 1981.

69. Ibid.; Robert H. Williams, testimony before the Subcommittee on Energy, Nu-

in a report of an energy R & D advisory board to the Reagan administration. Its conclusions are discussed in the following section.

Energy Research Advisory Board

In the continuing debate over the major redirections instituted in energy R & D by the Reagan administration, the report of the Department of Energy's Energy Research Advisory Board (ERAB) is noteworthy. It sparks interest because of its substantive recommendations and because of the composition and history of the board.

ERAB is composed of private citizens, including economists, scientists, corporate executives of energy companies, and representative environmental organization and consumer groups. In 1981 the board was an amalgam of holdovers from the Carter administration and a substantial number of new members appointed by the incoming Reagan administration. Thus it was broadly representative both in political terms and in terms of the questions and controversies that are inherent in the formulation of energy policy. In August 1981, the Department of Energy requested that the board review all federal energy R & D programs and establish priorities. The board presented its conclusions to the Energy Department in November 1981.[70]

Overall Philosophy. In introductory background sections of the report, the board acknowledged that the Carter and Reagan administrations approached energy R & D policy from quite different premises about the role of government. The Carter administration "defined an expansive role for federally-sponsored R & D, including demonstration and commercialization." The Reagan administration, however, "shifted the emphasis from federal sponsorship to reliance on the private sector," limiting the federal role to basic energy R & D, high-risk energy R & D, and research on health and environmental effects of energy usage. In addition, it said that the Reagan administration was determined to reduce federal expenditures and the federal deficit.

The board accepted the Reagan administration's philosophy and approach to energy R & D policy. It said: "ERAB's deliberations have reflected an expectation that federal funds will be stringently limited for the foreseeable future." It added that it "applauds the greater reliance on the private sector whenever possible" and "believes that

clear Proliferation, and Government Processes of the Senate Committee on Governmental Affairs, July 21, 1981.

70. Department of Energy, *Federal Energy R & D Priorities* (Report of the Research and Development Panel, Energy Research Advisory Board, Washington, D.C., November 1981), pp. iv–v and apps. A, B, C, and D.

much, perhaps most, of new energy supplies and greater efficiency in energy use will in fact be achieved by higher energy prices."[71]

The board went on to state that it was "concerned that some energy R & D of great potential significance . . . will fall between federal and industry responsibilities." To illustrate, ERAB first emphasized what it took to be the Reagan administration's position that basic research was primarily a federal responsibility. Beyond basic research, however, there were circumstances that would make complete assumption of industry responsibility difficult. The board noted, for example, that "some of the markets in which energy is sold are not 'free,' " namely the electric and gas utilities. In these regulated industries, it said, energy is priced so far below replacement cost that the gas and electric utilities can hardly afford additions to capacity, much less "expensive R & D." These utilities "have weak incentives to spend on R & D." Further, it said, some energy-related industries, such as the building industry, are "too fragmented to organize and finance a strong R & D response to market signals." Even among industries that are less fragmented and economically stronger, there are difficulties, because "industries with a strong R & D orientation and capability are the exceptions in America."[72]

Thus, ERAB concluded, in response to the Reagan administration's ideological bent toward a limited government role:

> ERAB in its evaluations of programs has taken the new policies and guidelines relative to the federal role very seriously, but ERAB has made exceptions where there is reasonable certainty that timely and adequate response by industry and commerce is an unrealistic assumption and that continued federal research support is therefore still required, at least for a time.[73]

Conclusions and Recommendations. ERAB took as its base document the Reagan administration's fiscal 1982 energy R & D budget proposals (original March figures). It divided energy R & D into four groups: electric supply; fuel (gas and liquid) supply; conservation and utilization; and science and technology base. (See appendix C for a summary of the ERAB recommendation.)

Electric supply. The board noted that though "no correct balance among energy forms and resources can be defined a priori, R & D for electric supply technology is receiving a larger proportion of funding than the present and projected share of electricity in our national

71. Ibid., pp. 5–6.
72. Ibid., pp. 6–7.
73. Ibid., p. 7.

98

energy supplies." Thus there were a number of electric-supply-related R & D programs that should have a "low priority and whose funding should either be substantially reduced or terminated." It added that "within electricity, federally sponsored nuclear programs are receiving a larger proportion of funding than the expected nuclear share of the U.S. energy mix during the next few decades."[74]

Regarding specific nuclear programs, the board recommended increased funding for nuclear waste disposal (particularly an accelerated demonstration schedule), uranium enrichment, and research to increase the efficiency and safety of existing light-water reactors. ERAB also declared fusion was "of long-term importance" and required the "maintenance of a substantial level of federal R & D funding" for years to come. It said, however, that a stretched-out fusion R & D program was possible if budget pressures demanded.[75]

On the liquid metal fast breeder reactor, the board recommended that the baseline R & D program continue to be a priority, but also held that "construction of a demonstration plant in the early 1980s is not an urgent national priority." It concluded:

> Sufficient coal and uranium supplies exist to satisfy projected levels of electrical demand for at least forty years and possibly well beyond. For these reasons, the panel recommends continued R & D on the liquid metal breeder reactor, as well as on other breeder concepts, but that demonstration of breeder technology be delayed until a future time.[76]

There were a number of nonnuclear electric programs that the board judged to be less deserving of federal support, either because their payoff potential was not large or because they were advanced enough for market forces to govern into the energy supply. These included solar power technology (wind and ocean energy), electric transmission systems, geothermal energy, magnetohydrodynamics, and hydropower.[77]

Liquid and gas supply R & D programs. In this area, the board followed the general guidelines for federal support that were laid down by the Reagan administration. It stated that

> the major federal effort in synthetic fuels research and development should be directed at innovative concepts at the laboratory and small pilot-plant scale with particular emphasis toward exploring a wider range of technological options

74. Ibid., pp. 14, 40.
75. Ibid., pp. 18–21.
76. Ibid., pp. 19–21, 43.
77. Ibid., pp. 21–22, 44.

with potential for significant efficiency and cost improvements. . . . [Federal funds for] large-scale demonstration projects involving substantial cost-shared federal outlays are not necessary or appropriate.

It should be noted that because of the limited nature of its mandate, ERAB did not tackle the question of the appropriateness of the Synthetic Fuels Corporation. It merely assumed the continued existence of that body and found this to be another reason that no Energy Department funds should be used for large-scale synthetic fuels demonstration programs.[78]

The board endorsed the reductions made by the Reagan administration in the biomass and alcohol fuels programs and agreed with the administration that support for techniques and processes to enhance oil and gas recovery should be left to the private sector. Finally, it recommended termination of federal funding for oil shale recovery programs, because the private sector was pursuing development in this area.[79]

Conservation and utilization R & D. The board clearly disagreed with the Reagan administration on conservation, concluding that

relative to their potential contributions to the solution of near- and medium-term energy problems, there is an imbalance in the allocation of R & D funds between conservation programs and those directed at supply. The budget needs a reordering of priorities to reflect better the opportunities that exist for efficiency improvements and the unique federal role in conservation R & D.[80]

Among the conservation programs, ERAB assigned the highest federal priority to buildings and community systems. It argued that "a federal role is highly appropriate in this field" because the building and construction industries are "fragmented and undercapitalized" and private sector R & D is "rare." Reducing energy consumption, particularly oil consumption, makes this an attractive investment for public funds. ERAB recommended, therefore, that "funding levels in this area be increased, emphasizing R & D that the private sector is not funding (particularly in retrofit and remodeling older buildings), while maintaining active R & D and technology transfer programs involving industry."[81]

78. Ibid., pp. 23–27, 44.
79. Ibid., pp. 26–28, 44.
80. Ibid., p. 29.
81. Ibid.

The board followed similar reasoning in calling for increased funding for the Energy Department's industrial process conservation programs. Although it admitted that high energy prices were providing strong incentives for all industries to conserve energy, it also found that many industries

> lack the ability to conduct R & D either because of their fragmented industrial structure or because of historical failure to support research. This appears to be true of many small and medium-sized businesses that, in the aggregate, consume large amounts of energy. Short-term high-payoff R & D will not be conducted unless federal leadership is given.

In this case, as in the case of building conservation programs, ERAB's conclusions opposed the Reagan administration's principle that energy price increases alone would produce significant reductions in energy consumption.[82] The board generally approved the Reagan administration's reductions in transportation conservation (including phaseout of electric and hybrid vehicle R & D), solar applications for buildings (largely photovoltaics), and solar applications for industrial processes.[83]

Science and technology base. The board recommended increased federal funding for a number of basic research programs, giving high priority to the effect of new energy technologies on the environment and health. It recommended more R & D on the long-range effect of the increased use of fossil fuels, specifically on the effect of increased CO_2 in the atmosphere and on the causes and effects of acid rain.[84]

Energy Program Reorganization

In its plan to reorganize the energy programs of the federal government, the Reagan administration broke with the three previous administrations. Presidents Nixon, Ford, and Carter, though the details of their proposals differed somewhat, all had called for consolidating energy programs into a cabinet-level department. Congress, in response, in 1977 created the Department of Energy, bringing together under one roof most federal energy R & D programs, federal energy regulatory programs, the nuclear weapons program, the strategic petroleum reserve, and a group of government-owned hydroelectric facilities.

82. Ibid., p. 32.
83. Ibid., p. 31.
84. Ibid., pp. 35–40.

Ronald Reagan, during the campaign of 1980, repeatedly pledged to abolish the Department of Energy, and in December 1981 the Reagan administration proposed that about 70 percent of DOE's activities be transferred to the Department of Commerce, including all of the energy R & D programs and the nuclear weapons programs. Energy R & D and nuclear weapons R & D would be united into the Energy Research and Technology Agency (ERTA), which would report directly to the secretary of commerce.[85] The Department of Interior would inherit the strategic petroleum reserve and the government's hydroelectric facilities. Federal energy regulatory activities would be spun off into an independent commission.

It was by no means certain that Congress would go along with President Reagan's plan, which went beyond questions of efficient and rational organization and reflected fundamental policy redirections. As Colin Norman, of *Science,* said:

> the bureaucratic move does more than fulfill a campaign pledge; it reflects the administration's view that the marketplace rather than the federal government should establish patterns of energy supply and demand. Energy, the argument goes, does not warrant a cabinet post of its own.[86]

The Fiscal 1983 Research and Development Budget

An economic recession and the prospect of an unprecedented deficit formed the background to the fiscal 1983 federal budget. Thus it was not surprising when President Reagan proposed to cut back sharply the rate of increase in all nondefense federal spending. Within the total federal budget of $757.6 billion, Reagan asked for a $27 billion cut in scheduled increases in domestic spending and a $33.6 billion increase in defense spending. Within the domestic program areas, $14.2 billion in cuts came from discretionary spending, a significant portion of which consists of R & D programs. Federal R & D programs, however, fared quite well.[87]

The Reagan administration proposed $43.0 billion in obligations for the conduct of R & D in fiscal 1983, an increase of $4.2 billion, or 10.8 percent, over the amount appropriated by Congress in fiscal 1982. Taking into account the administration's projected inflation rates for calendar years 1982 and 1983, this was a real increase over inflation

85. Colin Norman, "Commerce to Inherit Energy Research," *Science,* January 8, 1982, pp. 147–49.

86. Ibid., p. 147.

87. *New York Times,* February 6, 1982; *Wall Street Journal,* February 7, 1982; *Newsweek,* February 15, 1982; Colin Norman et al., "Science Budget: Coping with Austerity," *Science,* February 19, 1982, pp. 944–47.

of about 4 percent. Much of the R & D increase went to defense, which in fiscal 1983 constituted more than 60 percent of all federal R & D spending. Space and basic research also received important boosts. Energy R & D, however, continued the decline begun in the fiscal 1982 budget (table 7).[88]

The fiscal 1983 R & D budget reflected the dominant themes and revised priorities of the Reagan administration: protection of basic research; withdrawal of federal support for most large-scale civilian demonstration projects, particularly in energy; and continuation of a massive shift of resources into defense research and development.

OMB Rationale. The special analysis on R & D, which accompanied the fiscal 1983 budget, was the first OMB special R & D analysis bearing the full imprint of Reagan administration OMB appointees. It was combined, as always, with the residual views and institutional memory of the OMB professional staff. The analysis, *Special Analysis K: Research and Development*, was more detailed than its predecessors and had been clearly constructed to delineate and underscore several underlying precepts guiding federal R & D policy under the Reagan administration.

The document said that two categories of R & D activities were supported by the federal government:

- federal government needs—where the government itself was the sole or primary user of the results and products, as in defense or environmental regulation
- national needs—where the federal government intervened through R & D support on behalf of the economy or the general welfare in such areas as agriculture, health, and energy

Regarding national needs, however, *Special Analysis K* said that the "1983 budget reflects a clearer delineation than has been the case in the past between the responsibilities of the federal government and those of the private sector." Specifically, the federal government acknowledged two main responsibilities regarding R & D to meet national needs:

- First, it must provide an overall economic climate that encouraged innovation and private sector R & D investment. The administration's tax, budget, and regulatory policies were aimed to fulfill that responsibility.

88. Office of Management and Budget, *Special Analysis K: Research and Development* (Washington, D.C., February 1982), p. 5 (hereafter cited as OMB, *Special Analysis K*). The Reagan administration forecasts an inflation rate of 6.1 percent in calendar year 1982 and 7.9 percent in calendar year 1983: *New York Times*, February 6, 1981.

TABLE 7

CONDUCT OF RESEARCH AND DEVELOPMENT, BY MAJOR DEPARTMENTS AND AGENCIES, 1981–1983
(millions of dollars)

Department or Agency	Obligations			Outlays		
	1981 actual	1982 estimate	1983 estimate	1981 actual	1982 estimate	1983 estimate
Defense-military functions	16,494	20,553	24,469	15,720	18,784	22,673
National Aeronautics and Space Administration	5,407	5,841	6,513	5,279	5,696	6,460
Commerce	5,276	4,793	4,157	5,466	5,240	4,352
Energy Research and Technology Administration[a]	(4,948)	(4,522)	(3,917)	(5,121)	(4,948)	(4,104)
Health and Human Services	3,973	3,972	4,122	3,991	3,935	4,039
National Institutes of Health	(3,332)	(3,427)	(3,533)	(3,350)	(3,390)	(3,487)
National Science Foundation	964	961	1,033	892	1,018	908
Agriculture	773	807	838	742	805	824
Interior	424	397	371	438	402	380
Transportation	420	329	366	418	321	316
Environmental Protection Agency	326	317	230	344	335	274
Nuclear Regulatory Commission	227	223	220	211	209	206
Agency for International Development	156	160	186	151	157	159
Veterans Administration	147	137	145	138	130	140
Education	91	74	76	96	94	112
All other[b]	354	279	272	366	298	280
Total conduct of R & D	35,033	38,843	42,997	34,252	37,425	41,122

NOTE: Detail may not add to totals because of rounding.
a. Assumes that Congress will agree to the Reagan administration's proposal to abolish the Department of Energy.
b. Includes the Departments of Housing and Urban Development, Justice, Labor, Treasury, and State, the Tennessee Valley Authority, the Smithsonian Institution, the Corps of Engineers, the Federal Emergency Management Agency, the U.S. Office of Personnel Management, the Library of Congress, the Arms Control and Disarmament Agency, the Federal Communications Commission, the Advisory Committee on Intergovernmental Relations, and the Federal Trade Commission.
SOURCE: Office of Management and Budget.

- Second, it must provide direct R & D support only where there was "substantial prospect for significant economic gain for the nation but where the private sector is unlikely to invest adequately . . .

because the benefits, in large measure, are not immediately 'appropriable,' by individual firms."

Thus the federal government supported basic research but "limits its spending on technology development to technologies requiring a long period of initial development, such as fusion power, where the risk is high but the payoff to the Nation is potentially large."[89]

Basic Research. For fiscal 1983, the Reagan administration proposed $5.8 billion for the conduct of basic research, an increase of 9 percent over the $5.3 billion appropriated by Congress in fiscal 1982. Using the inflation rate projected by the administration for 1982 and 1983, this allows for a 2–3 percent real increase in the support of basic research in fiscal 1983 (see table 8).[90]

Among individual agencies, the National Institutes of Health provided the largest amount of basic research support ($1.9 billion). It was followed by NSF ($984 million); DOD ($781 million); the Commerce Department, which will, according to the administration plan, inherit all energy R & D ($762 million); NASA ($682 million); and the Agriculture Department ($359 million).[91]

Basic research priorities. Like the Reagan administration's fiscal 1982 R & D budget, the fiscal 1983 R & D budget granted higher priority to physical and natural sciences than to social and behavioral sciences. The OMB special analysis on R & D said: "Basic research in such fields as chemistry, physics, biology, materials oceanography, and earth sciences provides the underpinning . . . for advances in health care, improved nutrition and agricultural production, and new technologies for defense, space and energy." In addition, it said that "special emphasis [was] also being given . . . to strengthening basic research in the physical sciences and engineering," because "such areas of research are of particular importance to long-term productivity and economic growth."[92]

The internal priorities of the NSF basic research allotment reflected the underlying precepts of the OMB special analysis. NSF received $984 million for the conduct of basic research programs in fiscal 1983, up 7.8 percent from the $912 million in fiscal 1982.[93]

Within the total NSF basic research budget, the largest increases were in the mathematical and physical sciences, engineering science,

89. OMB, *Special Analysis K*, pp. 3–4.
90. Ibid., pp. 6–7.
91. Ibid.
92. Ibid.
93. Ibid.

TABLE 8

CONDUCT OF BASIC RESEARCH, BY MAJOR DEPARTMENTS AND AGENCIES, 1981–1983
(millions of dollars)

Department or Agency	Obligations			Outlays		
	1981 actual	1982 estimate	1983 estimate	1981 actual	1982 estimate	1983 estimate
Health and Human Services	1,955	2,000	2,069	1,944	1,978	2,034
National Institutes of Health	(1,767)	(1,839)	(1,897)	(1,750)	(1,813)	(1,869)
National Science Foundation	898	912	984	830	972	861
Defense-military functions	603	673	781	554	616	712
Commerce	608	665	762	614	670	759
Energy Research and Technology Administration[a]	(591)	(647)	(741)	(597)	(652)	(737)
National Aeronautics and Space Administration	532	580	682	538	575	661
Agriculture	314	332	359	302	337	354
Interior	80	73	68	79	73	69
Smithsonian Institution	44	45	51	41	44	51
Veterans Administration	15	13	14	15	13	14
Education	17	14	14	18	18	22
Environmental Protection Agency	10	15	10	12	12	10
All other[b]	32	27	28	29	29	28
Total	5,108	5,348	5,821	4,975	5,337	5,574

NOTES: The amounts reported in this table are included in totals for conduct of R & D. Detail may not add to totals because of rounding.
a. Assumes that Congress will agree to the Reagan administration's proposal to abolish the Department of Energy.
b. Includes the Departments of Justice, Transportation, Treasury, and Labor, the Tennessee Valley Authority, the Corps of Engineers, the Federal Trade Commission, the Library of Congress, and the Agency for International Development.
SOURCE: Office of Management and Budget.

and earth science. The mathematical and physical sciences increased 9.5 percent, from $272.9 million in fiscal 1982 to $298.7 million in fiscal 1983. Basic engineering projects received $99.7 million in fiscal 1983— 9.8 percent more than in fiscal 1982. The combined areas of astronomical, atmospheric, earth, and ocean sciences received $259.7 million in fiscal 1983, an 8.2 percent increase over the $240.0 million in fiscal 1982.[94]

94. National Science Foundation, *Statement of FY 1983 Budget* (Washington, D.C.,

The biological, behavioral, and social sciences increased by 6.1 percent over fiscal 1982, from $176.0 million to $186.7 million. Social and economic science, however, went up only 1.1 percent, reflecting the lower priority the Reagan administration continued to give these research areas.[95]

Several other NSF programs were also scheduled for decreased funding. Science and engineering education activities, which had received a major cut between fiscal 1981 and fiscal 1982, continued to drop—from $20.9 million in fiscal 1982 to $15.0 million in fiscal 1983, a decrease of over 28 percent. Ocean drilling programs dropped 30 percent—from $20.0 million in fiscal 1982 to $14.0 million in fiscal 1983. This decrease reflected the decision to abandon the Ocean Margin Drilling Project, which had been given high priority by the Carter administration. The Reagan administration said that crucial industry support for it had not been forthcoming.[96]

Space. After protracted and difficult negotiations and internal debate, the Reagan administration granted substantial relief from the extreme budget pinch that had bound the space agency for the past several years. In fiscal 1983, the president's budget called for obligations for the conduct of R & D by NASA to increase to $6.5 billion, or $0.7 billion more than in fiscal 1982. Much of the increase would help make the space shuttle system fully operational. The increase also continued other space R & D, particularly a number of space science projects that had been in peril during the entire negotiations over the fiscal 1983 NASA budget. In keeping with the overall rationale of the fiscal 1983 R & D budget, which foresaw a larger role for the private sector in funding appropriable research, both space applications and aeronautical R & D received lower priority. Finally, no new space projects were funded in fiscal 1983.[97]

Space shuttle. In fiscal 1983, NASA's space transportation systems (largely the space shuttle) were scheduled to receive $3.5 billion, about 55 percent of the total space agency budget. The increase of almost $400 million for space shuttle activities would be spent for the transition to a fully operational system; for demonstration of the use of the shuttle to repair a damaged satellite in orbit; for enhancement of the payload lift of the shuttle; for continued procurement of a second spacelab for scientific experiments in space; and for continued

February 8, 1982), pp. 4–5, and accompanying tables appended.

95. Ibid.

96. Ibid., pp. 5–6 and accompanying tables; Norman et al., "Science Budget," p. 945.

97. OMB, *Special Analysis K*, pp. 5, 10.

development of an upper stage for the shuttle to be used in high-earth orbit and interplanetary missions.[98]

Space science. For conduct of space science R & D in fiscal 1983, the NASA budget proposed $682 million, $114 million more than the $568 million provided by Congress in fiscal 1982. With one exception (the Venus Orbiting Imaging Radar project, which was canceled), this increase allowed all existing major space science projects to continue, though no new ones were announced. The fiscal 1983 space science budget supported:

- the space telescope, planned for launch in 1985
- the Gamma Ray Observatory, planned for launch in 1988
- the Galileo mission to Jupiter, to be launched in 1985
- Spacelab astronomy experiments as a part of the first Spacelab project, to be launched in 1983
- a number of experiments to be conducted through use of smaller satellites, balloons, and aircraft[99]

Space and terrestial applications. The Reagan administration proposed to spend $320 million for space and terrestial applications in fiscal 1983, slightly less than the $334 million provided by Congress in fiscal 1982. The space and terrestial applications budget supported completion of the LANDSAT-D series of satellites, which use space remote-sensing technology to study earth resources. It also provided for other programs to improve the understanding of the earth's climate, weather, and pollution. Basic research in materials science through low-gravity experiments was to be supported as a part of Spacelab's activities.[100]

Aeronautical research and technology programs. Aeronautical R & D in NASA was also scheduled for a slight decrease in fiscal 1983—from $233 million in fiscal 1982 to $232 million in fiscal 1983. The OMB special analysis of the fiscal 1983 R & D budget said that support for aeronautical R & D would focus more on fundamental basic research and "technology development and demonstration projects with relatively near-term commercial applications would be curtailed as an inappropriate federal subsidy."[101]

In fiscal 1983, NASA aeronautical priorities will be placed on aerodynamics, propulsion, and avionics and on flight controls and human-vehicle interaction.

98. Ibid., p. 11.
99. Ibid., pp. 11–12; Norman et al., "Science Budget," p. 947.
100. OMB, *Special Analysis K,* pp. 12–13.
101. Ibid., p. 13.

Defense. Under the Reagan administration's proposals, obligations for defense-related R & D (derived from DOD and Commerce [Energy] Department programs) would come to $26.2 billion in fiscal 1983, an increase of 19 percent over the $22 billion in obligations provided by Congress in fiscal 1982. This would bring defense R & D to almost 61 percent of total federal R & D obligations for fiscal 1983.[102]

Technology base, basic research. In technology base (consisting of basic research, advanced exploratory research, and advanced technology development categories), the increase from fiscal 1982 to fiscal 1983 would be $600 million, from $3.6 billion provided by Congress in fiscal 1982 to $4.2 billion proposed by the Reagan administration in fiscal 1983. Basic research alone would increase from $673 million in fiscal 1982 to $781 million in fiscal 1983.

Among the high-priority technology base research areas and programs singled out by the OMB in fiscal 1983 were very high speed integrated circuits, guided munitions capable of being operational in adverse weather, improved information processing, improved sensors, advanced computer languages, advanced materials research, and methods of computing high-power lasers.[103]

Strategic programs. Defense R & D related to strategic programs increased from $4.8 billion in fiscal 1982 to $6.5 billion in fiscal 1983. The increases provided for accelerated development of ballistic missile defense, including exploration of options for MX missile basing, for continued development of an antisatellite system, for an advanced-technology bomber, and for increased emphasis on the development of communications and control systems needed to support the entire array of strategic weapons.[104]

Tactical programs. Defense R & D related to tactical programs increased from $7 billion in fiscal 1982 to $7.5 billion in fiscal 1983. For the army, this included funds to improve the M-1 tank, chemical defense equipment, a number of new helicopter systems, and continued development of the Patriot antiaircraft missile system. For the air force, this included funds for advanced versions of the F-15 and F-16 fighters and for the AMRAAM advanced medium-range air-to-air missile. For the navy, this included development of a lightweight antisubmarine torpedo, a new destroyer, and a vertical launch system for missiles.[105]

102. Ibid., pp. 5, 8.
103. Ibid., pp. 8–9.
104. Ibid., p. 9.
105. Ibid.

Intelligence and communications. These programs increased from $2.2 billion in fiscal 1982 to $2.7 billion in fiscal 1983. R & D was focused on communications satellites, on radios that would function in the electronic noise of the battlefield, and on battlefield surveillance radars.[106]

Energy R & D. The Reagan administration's fiscal 1983 energy R & D proposals assumed that Congress would approve its proposal to dismantle the Department of Energy and transfer all energy R & D programs to a new Energy Research and Technology Administration (ERTA) in the Department of Commerce. The administration proposed $2.0 billion for the conduct of energy R & D (this includes ERTA and Nuclear Regulatory Commission R & D) in fiscal 1983, down from $2.8 billion in fiscal 1982. The administration also proposed $224 million for energy R & D facilities.

In the fiscal 1983 budget, the administration continued to pursue three policy shifts that it had begun to implement in the fiscal 1982 budget: withdrawal of the federal government from support of large-scale energy demonstration projects and R & D that had appropriable results for the private sector; an increased emphasis on energy production over energy conservation; and within the energy production sector, a sharp tilt toward nuclear energy. Regarding nuclear energy, R & D in direct support of nuclear programs was scheduled to receive 66 percent of all energy R & D funds in the fiscal 1983 budget.[107]

Energy R & D related to production received almost 100 percent of all energy R & D funds. Energy conservation R & D was scheduled for just $18 million in fiscal 1983.

Nuclear fission, fusion programs. The proposed R & D budget for nuclear fission programs in fiscal 1983 was $1.0 billion, down from $1.1 billion in fiscal 1982. Breeder reactor systems (largely the liquid metal fast breeder reactor program) would receive $577 million. A funding level of $444 million was proposed for magnetic fusion R & D, up slightly from $435 million in fiscal 1982.[108]

Fossil fuels. In fiscal 1983, the Reagan administration proposed to withdraw from fossil fuel R & D almost entirely, asking only $107 million for the conduct of fossil energy R & D and for supporting facilities. Congress had provided $417 million for these programs in

106. Ibid.

107. Ibid., pp. 5, 14–15, 26; Department of Energy, *Federal Energy Programs, FY 1983 Budget Highlights* (Washington, D.C., February 1982), pp. 7–8 (hereafter cited as DOE, *Budget Highlights*); Norman et al., "Science Budget," p. 947.

108. DOE, *Budget Highlights*, pp. 8–12.

fiscal 1982 and $994 million in fiscal 1981. The Department of Energy, in the fiscal 1983 budget analysis, explained the administration's action on fossil fuel R & D:

> As a result of the administration's action last year to decontrol the price of oil, government subsidies and regulations which reduced production and encouraged oil imports have been abandoned, and free market forces have greatly increased the attractiveness of domestic energy investments.
>
> The Fossil Energy budget reflects this changing role of the federal government. The process began last year, when the Fossil Energy budget was realigned to concentrate on long-term, high-risk research and development, while relying on the private sector to demonstrate and commercialize promising individual technologies and processes. This year, the concept of supporting long-term, technology development has been refined. In fiscal 1983, long-term, research and development *intended to accelerate the development of advanced technologies* [italics added] will not be conducted, and almost all proof-of-concept work will be left to industry to complete. Again, it is the role of the private sector, responding to free market forces, to support and accelerate advanced technology development.

As for basic fossil fuel research, priority was to be given to flame research, coal structure, catalysis, and kinetics.[109]

Solar and other renewable energy sources. Solar and other renewable energy sources R & D was proposed at a level of $83 million, down dramatically from the $248 million provided by Congress in fiscal 1982. Within this total, individual reductions came in photovoltaic energy systems ($74 million in fiscal 1982; $27 million in fiscal 1983); biomass energy systems ($53 million in fiscal 1982; $18 million in fiscal 1983); wind energy systems ($34 million in fiscal 1982; $5 million in fiscal 1983); ocean energy systems ($19 million in fiscal 1982; $0 in fiscal 1983); and alcohol fuels ($10 million in fiscal 1982; $3 million in fiscal 1983).

In addition, geothermal energy R & D was cut from $53 million in fiscal 1982 to $10 million in fiscal 1983 and electrical energy and storage systems from $58 million in fiscal 1982 to $0 in fiscal 1983.

In explaining the large cuts in the solar and other renewable energy sources R & D budgets, the Energy Department's budget analysis echoed the reasoning put forward for fossil fuel R & D:

The administration's policies for solar energy continue the

109. Ibid., pp. 15–17.

redirection begun last year to place greater emphasis on the private sector, not federal programs, in developing and commercializing solar technologies. By relying on the marketplace and private industry, it is no longer necessary for the federal government to support the development, demonstration and commercialization of solar energy, including R & D undertaken for the purpose of accelerating the introduction of new solar technologies. The free market will determine the development and introduction rates of solar technologies consistent with their economic potential.[110]

Energy conservation. The Department of Energy defended the almost total withdrawal of federal support for conservation R & D:

Efficient energy use is being effectively encouraged by rising energy costs and the Economic Recovery Program, thereby permitting a substantial curtailment in the federal conservation programs.

From a total of $144 billion in fiscal 1982 (including $63 million in deferred spending from fiscal 1981), conservation R & D was directed toward basic research in such areas as heat transfer and fluid mechanics, energy-conserving materials (particularly ceramics) and processes, thermochemical conservation, and electrochemistry.[111]

110. Ibid., pp. 19–22.
111. Ibid., pp. 18–19.

5
Policy Recommendations

What follows is a group of five policy recommendations. In two cases—the recommendations regarding basic research and those relating to the government's role in demonstration and commercialization—the proposals attempt to achieve a more rigorous adherence to the rationale and consensus that have evolved during the Ford, Carter, and Reagan administrations regarding the federal government's role in support of R & D. In both cases, also, the specific recommendations are tailored to fit the tight fiscal conditions that are likely to obtain for the foreseeable future. The other three recommendations relate to long-range planning, federal science organization, and the implications of the increasingly dominant role of defense R & D. Based on judgments flowing from the overall research and analysis that went into the monograph, they are an attempt to anticipate emerging issues and problems in the federal R & D enterprise.

Basic Research

In the future, the primary attention and concern of the White House and Congress should be redirected toward the long-term, basic research elements of the federal research and development budget. There should be less attention and concern focused on swings in the applied end of the R & D spectrum. Prudence would also dictate that the federal basic research budget should grow each year at a rate that matches inflation—and, when possible, allows for a small real increase.

This proposal logically follows from an agreement that has developed over several decades—and has been strongly reaffirmed by the Ford, Carter, and Reagan administrations—that the private sector will not support basic research at an adequate level. It will not do so because individual firms cannot retain many of the benefits from the research; because of the risk and uncertainty of the timing of the benefits; and in some cases because there is the need for huge, long-term investment. Only the federal government can serve as the balance wheel to ensure an adequate level of national spending for

113

research to advance general scientific knowledge.

The proposal is also responsive to the political and fiscal climate. Basic research is less costly than projects at the demonstration, development, and commercialization end of the R & D spectrum. Of the total R & D budget of almost $40 billion in fiscal 1982, basic research programs cost about $5.3 billion, or just over 13 percent. Thus, small absolute increases in basic research exercise a high leveraging effect.

Admittedly, there are no exact criteria for establishing the adequacy of the federal basic research budget. Acknowledging the paucity of hard evidence to support any particular level of federal support, the proposal builds on the experience of the federal science support system over the past decade and a half. It reflects the conviction that basic scientific progress depends on steady, enduring, and adequate support, free from abrupt swings and redirections. Because of the nature of the research process, instability and unpredictability can have devastating consequences. It often takes years to assemble research teams that are both intellectually and personally compatible. And once dismantled, they are not easily or quickly reassembled. Furthermore, advances in scientific disciplines depend upon a continuing infusion of young minds from the graduate schools and universities, and without some ability to plan a research agenda it is impossible to attract talent into individual research projects. Finally, increasingly, in physics, in biology, and in other disciplines, laboratory equipment and facilities—accelerators, spacecraft, oceanography vessels—are becoming enormously expensive to build and operate; and an on-again, off-again science support system results in wasteful, inefficient use of these costly resources.

Government Role in Demonstration and Commercialization Projects

Office of Management and Budget (OMB) officials in the Ford and Carter administrations tried with mixed success to move the federal government out of the business of funding large-scale demonstration and commercialization projects. The Reagan administration has more zealously than the two preceding administrations followed the logic of its own theories concerning the proper role at the "D" end of the R & D spectrum; however, the Reagan administration should continue to examine its budget priorities for contradictions to these theories, and revise them accordingly.

Energy. Because of the huge sums of money involved, the most glaring contradictions to the Reagan administration's professed ad-

114

herence to free-market principles and to the application of "sound criteria" in place of the "current subsidy programs" are the Clinch River demonstration plant and the projected $17 billion subsidy for the construction of synthetic fuel plants by private industry.

The CRBR has cost $1.1 billion up to 1981, and will cost at least $2.2 billion more before construction is complete in 1988. Observers and commentators from a wide political and ideological spectrum—from David Stockman and the Heritage Foundation on the right to environmentalists on the left—have denounced construction of this plant. Further, the Energy Research Advisory Board (ERAB), which supported the base breeder research program, has also recommended that "demonstration of the breeder technology be delayed until a future time." Cancellation of the plant construction would free more than $2 billion in the next four or five fiscal years and open the potential for reprogramming of scarce federal dollars toward basic research or to other applied research and demonstration programs of higher priority.

Unlike money for the breeder demonstration, the $17 billion subsidies authorized for synthetic fuel plants are off budget and flow directly to the Synthetic Fuels Corporation from the excess profits oil tax. The provision of these large subsidies, however, contradicts the Reagan administration's own stringent rules concerning government intervention to subsidize technical or commercial demonstrations. Thus, the Synthetic Fuels Corporation will inevitably overtake activities of the private sector, make judgments regarding technological promise and economic viability that are best left to the private sector, and overinvest in similar technologies that promise only marginal improvements in energy production. All of these are traditional OMB cautions that have been heavily stressed by Reagan administration OMB political appointees. As with the breeder demonstration plant, the administration, despite the political difficulties, should consider abolishing the Synthetic Fuels Corporation or cutting back substantially the funds available to it for direct subsidies. It could then recommend that Congress reprogram some of the funds back into the nation's science support system.

In the energy conservation area, the decision to eliminate funding for R & D for conservation in buildings and for industrial processes should be reexamined in light of the arguments—particularly for the building industry—that even short-term, high-payoff R & D will not be done unless the government takes the lead. The Reagan administration has argued that increases in the cost of energy alone will force conservation measures—and investment in R & D to support those measures. But ERAB has pointed out that because of the fragmented nature of the building and construction industry (no one company has even 1 percent of the market, for instance), because the industry is undercapitalized, and because there is no tradition of research, R & D in product and design innovation will not be done.

ERAB also argued that the budget for industrial processes R & D should be increased. Here, one should proceed on an industry-by-industry basis, and the government should target funds only to those industries where there is clear-cut evidence that energy price increases are not producing R & D to increase the efficiency of processes and techniques.

A predisposition toward increased R & D for buildings and industry processes is buttressed by two other relevant facts: utilization and conservation programs constituted only 8 percent of the total fiscal 1982 energy R & D budget; and the amount of money is quite small compared with the large sums expended for individual projects on the energy supply side of the ledger (the Carter administration fiscal 1982 budget for building conservation R & D was only $53 million, and for industrial conservation only $67 million). Thus, as ERAB argued: "Relative to their potential contributions to the solution of the near- and medium-term energy problems, there is an imbalance in the allocation of R & D funds between the conservation programs and those directed at supply."

Space. If continuing downward pressure on the NASA budget forces severe cutbacks or cancellation of whole program areas, space science should have priority over the aeronautics or space application programs. The situation with regard to space science is a subset of the issues described above regarding basic research in general. Short-term cutbacks here, as across the entire basic research effort, will have long-run, possibly irretrievable costs. Further, as the Heritage Foundation argued, aeronautics is an area where "the benefits of an innovation are sufficiently appropriable that the private sector should be counted on to invest in the innovation." If there are particular defense aeronautical needs and requirements, then the air force, not NASA, should be funding them. Regarding space applications, the issue becomes "how much the nation can afford and when." Postponing or stretching out programs to put another agricultural or mineral survey satellite into orbit would do much less harm in the long term than dismantling basic space science research teams.

Longer-Range Planning

Predictability is as important as stability in ensuring the continuing health of basic scientific research. During its first year in office, one of the most damaging aspects of the Reagan administration's treatment of federal science and technology was a lack of communication concerning its real priorities and its long-range plans. As William D. Carey, executive officer of the AAAS, said: "We seem to be in for an extended period of retrenchment for federal R & D, but what I don't see—and what worries me most—is any plan or overall strategy within the administration for how we get from here to there—how do we beat an orderly retreat if that is going to be necessary." Without introducing unwarranted rigidity, the Reagan administration could take the lead in expanding the political process to encompass a flexible commitment to longer-range funding for basic scientific disciplines. Longer-range funding decisions would also allow more "orderly retreats" from those areas deemed no longer of high priority.

Existing Mechanisms. The *Five Year Outlook* of the National Science Foundation (NSF), the annual report of the National Science Board, or the OMB special analyses that accompany each budget should be revised so that they lay out recommendations for basic research priorities over at least a five-year period. The White House, represented by the president's science adviser, after evaluating these and other outside recommendations, should at the time the president's budget is announced each year describe and update the administration's long-range plans for increasing, maintaining, or decreasing particular areas of basic research. In addition, Congress should move to multiyear authorizations for the basic research portions of the federal budget.

Federal R & D Organization

The time has come to take a hard look at the structure and organization of the federal R & D effort in light of changed conditions and future pressures. Rather than proceeding piecemeal, as it is doing with the proposed shift of energy R & D programs to the Commerce Department, the Reagan administration should undertake a full-scale review of the current organization of federal science and technology programs with the goal of recommending an optimum structure to meet the current pressures and future challenges.

There are a number of factors and conditions that make such a review timely. The Reagan administration, in defending the proposed transfer of energy R & D programs to the Commerce Department, stated that the chief reason for the choice was that the department already was responsible for several technology agencies, such as the National Bureau of Standards and the National Oceanic and Atmospheric Administration. With this rationale, does the administration

117

see this move as the first step toward consolidating a number of federal science and technology programs in what could emerge as a Department of Technology or a Department of Science and Technology? If this is the case, then what of the other quite different missions identified with Commerce—for instance, urban economic development? During the Carter administration, there was a major effort in the White House to transform Commerce into a Department of Urban and Economic Development. Conversely, both the Nixon and the Ford administrations argued that the most natural and sensible combination in the energy area was to link energy programs with natural resources programs. These administrations proposed a Department of Natural Resources, which would have been composed of most of the programs in the Department of Interior and the Department of Energy. The point here is not that either the Carter or the Nixon-Ford proposal was superior but that the Reagan administration's piecemeal approach has raised a number of larger unanswered questions.

Further, there are several other important organizational issues looming regarding the federal science and technology structure. As noted previously, NASA Administrator James M. Beggs has argued that within several years, NASA should plan to spin off the space shuttle into some kind of quasi-public, quasi-private independent organization like COMSAT. This would raise the question of what should become of the remaining NASA programs in space sciences and space applications. The National Science Foundation is also changing. Under the leadership of the National Science Board and under pressure from Congress, NSF is broadening its heavy emphasis on basic scientific research, also including significant funding for basic engineering research and more applied research. Finally, there are many questions concerning the national laboratories. George Keyworth, the president's science adviser, who is a product of the national laboratory system, is leading an interagency examination of the role of the national laboratories, but that role is also dependent on larger structural decisions in Washington.

Thus a confluence of factors, conditions, and pressures argue for a searching in-depth reexamination of the organization of the federal science and technology support system.

Defense R & D

The Reagan administration should commission a study by an independent, respected outside body of scientists—the National Academy of Sciences is the most likely candidate—of the implications of the reemergence of the Department of Defense (DOD) as the single most important federal R & D support agency.

In fiscal 1983, defense R & D will constitute over 60 percent of the total federal R & D budget. Since 1980, defense funding for basic research has risen more than 30 percent, a rate of increase that surpasses all other federal agencies and that brings DOD within a short distance of supplanting NSF as the chief across-the-board supporter of basic research. Defense R & D administrators have boldly moved to exploit their enhanced position. They have announced that the restrictive influence of the Mansfield Amendment is gone and that they will fund a wide spectrum of basic research projects. They are working to reestablish strong symbiotic connections with the nation's colleges and universities; and they are moving to fill perceived gaps in the science support system in areas such as education (graduate fellowships) and university laboratory instrumentation.

There is nothing inherently negative, and certainly nothing sinister or evil, about the reemergence of a strong role for the DOD in R & D. There are, however, a number of questions that arise from potential incongruities between its defense mission and its obligation to overall national scientific priorities and advancement. In basic research, for example, to what degree will projects supported by DOD be targeted and more narrowly constricted to defense goals, rather than being allowed a free flow of scientific discovery? To what degree will DOD increase the strong competition for the best young scientists in disciplines—such as information technology and high-energy physics—that it considers of top priority? And what will be the consequences of this competition for the nation at large? Finally, what about the movement, centered in the DOE and the CIA, to restrict the flow of scientific and technological information to the Soviet Union? To what degree will the Defense Department attempt to introduce restrictive requirements on DOD-supported basic research carried out in the nation's colleges and universities? In summary, while there are many advantages in increased defense support for R & D, there are also a number of potentially troubling issues that should be assessed and monitored.

Appendix A

The Structure of the Science Support System in the United States

Since 1945 the major sources for funding research and development activities have been the federal government and private industry, with colleges and universities and other nonprofit institutions making small contributions from their own funds. The actual performers of R & D during this time have been these same components plus a group of federally funded R & D centers, which are administered by individual universities, university consortia, federal laboratories, and other nonprofit research institutions.

In 1953, the first year of the Eisenhower administration, the total public and private investment in R & D was $5.1 billion; by 1980 it had grown to $61.1 billion (in constant 1972 dollars these totals would be $8.7 billion and $34.5 billion, respectively). The federal government provided 54 percent of the total R & D funds in 1953 and nonfederal sources 46 percent. The federal government's share of total R & D outlays grew steadily during the 1950s and early 1960s. In 1964 it reached a postwar high, totaling 66 percent of the nation's funding for scientific and technological projects. Since then the federal government has provided an ever-decreasing percentage of the total national outlay for R & D. Since the mid-1970s, both the federal and the nonfederal shares have hovered around 50 percent, but in the last three years (1979–1981) the federal share has dropped one percentage point and now stands at about 47 percent. (See table 9, on sources of R & D funds).[1]

Over the past three decades, each of the three main elements in the R & D process—basic research, applied research, and development—has experienced changing levels of support from federal and

1. National Science Foundation, *National Patterns of Science and Technology Resources, 1981* (Washington, D.C., 1981), pp. 25, 29 (hereafter cited as NSF, *National Patterns, 1981*). See also National Science Foundation, *Federal Funds for Research and Development, Fiscal Years 1979–81* (Washington, D.C., 1980), pp. 5–7 (hereafter cited as NSF, *Federal Funds, 1979–81*).

nonfederal sources. In addition, the actual performance of work by the components of the R & D universe—industry, universities, government laboratories—has shifted.

TABLE 9

SOURCES OF FUNDS FOR RESEARCH AND DEVELOPMENT,
BY SECTOR, 1953 AND 1960–1981
(millions of dollars)

Year	Total	Federal Government	Industry	Universities and Colleges	Other Nonprofit Institutions
Current dollars					
1953	5,124	2,753	2,245	72	54
1960	13,523	8,738	4,516	149	120
1961	14,316	9,250	4,757	165	144
1962	15,394	9,911	5,123	185	175
1963	17,059	11,204	5,456	207	192
1964	18,854	12,537	5,887	235	195
1965	20,044	13,012	6,548	267	217
1966	21,846	13,968	7,328	304	246
1967	23,146	14,395	8,142	345	264
1968	24,605	14,928	9,005	390	282
1969	25,631	14,895	10,010	420	306
1970	26,072	14,830	10,444	461	337
1971	26,653	14,941	10,822	529	361
1972	28,429	15,760	11,710	574	385
1973	30,665	16,346	13,293	613	413
1974	32,814	16,800	14,878	677	459
1975	35,169	18,065	15,820	749	535
1976	38,935	19,833	17,694	808	600
1977	42,923	21,674	19,696	881	672
1978	48,023	23,893	22,336	1,028	766
1979 (prelim.)	54,215	26,556	25,638	1,183	838
1980 (est.)	61,127	29,302	29,475	1,385	965
1981 (est.)	69,065	32,665	33,865	1,485	1,050

TABLE 9 (continued)

Year	Total	Federal Government	Industry	Universities and Colleges	Other Nonprofit Institutions
		Constant dollars			
1953	8,677	4,649	3,816	121	91
1960	19,635	12,673	6,573	214	175
1961	20,584	13,282	6,861	235	206
1962	21,750	13,989	7,256	259	246
1963	23,733	15,570	7,611	285	267
1964	25,857	17,179	8,090	320	268
1965	26,896	17,443	8,806	356	291
1966	28,442	18,180	9,547	395	320
1967	29,241	18,176	10,299	434	332
1968	29,833	18,108	10,910	474	341
1969	29,586	17,209	11,536	488	353
1970	28,545	16,248	11,421	506	370
1971	27,790	15,591	11,271	553	375
1972	28,429	15,760	11,710	574	385
1973	29,112	15,551	12,579	588	394
1974	28,755	14,798	12,947	605	405
1975	28,169	14,526	12,603	608	432
1976	29,499	15,038	13,393	613	455
1977	30,654	15,464	14,085	626	479
1978	32,010	15,928	14,886	685	511
1979 (prelim.)	33,304	16,312	15,751	727	514
1980 (est.)	34,499	16,551	16,619	784	545
1981 (est.)	35,457	16,781	17,373	763	540

NOTE: Constant dollars are based on GNP implicit price deflator.
SOURCE: National Science Foundation.

Basic Research

The federal government has remained the mainstay of support for basic research. Since the 1960s, it has provided about two-thirds of the total funds for projects to advance general scientific knowledge. National totals for basic research in real terms increased from the late 1950s until about 1968, then decreased 20 percent by 1975. From 1975 to 1980 (at least until President Reagan's 1981 budget changes), basic research increased annually at about 4 percent. Between 1980 and 1983, according to an analysis done by the AAAS, funds for basic research will have declined by 5.5 percent in real terms.[2]

Colleges and universities use half of all the basic research funds provided by federal grants. This came to just over $4 billion in 1980. The federal government and associated federally funded R & D centers perform another quarter of the basic research and industry and nonprofit institutions the rest.[3]

Applied Research

Historically, the vast bulk of the funds for applied research have been supplied by the federal government and industry, in that order. Throughout the 1960s and early 1970s, federal support for applied research averaged about 55 percent of the total funds committed to applied research in the United States, with industry support averaging just over 40 percent. During the 1970s, however, industry gradually moved to overtake the federal government as the chief supplier of funds for applied research, and much of the increased industry funding went for energy-related projects. From 1975 to 1980, industry's funds for applied research increased by 30 percent, while federal funds, reflecting a shift of emphasis from applied to basic research, increased by only 14 percent. In 1980 industry supplied 47 percent ($6.5 billion) of all the applied funds, and the federal government supplied 46 percent ($6.4 billion). One reason for the smaller increases in federal applied R & D was that NASA's applied research spending decreased, by 15 percent in real terms between 1976 and 1980.[4]

Although much of the funding came from the federal government, industry has always been the predominant performer of applied research. In 1960, for example, when total applied research funds came to about $3 billion, industry used $2 billion of it, the federal government $600 million, and universities and colleges $180 million. Similarly, in 1980, out of a total of $13.7 billion spent for

2. NSF, *National Patterns, 1981*, pp. 11–12; National Science Foundation, *National Patterns of Science and Technology Resources, 1980* (Washington, D.C., 1980), pp. 17–18 (hereafter cited as NSF, *National Patterns, 1980*).

3. NSF, *National Patterns, 1981*, p. 26.

4. NSF, *National Patterns, 1981;* see also National Science Foundation, *National Patterns of R & D Resources, 1953–1978-79* (Washington, D.C., 1978), pp. 8–9 (hereafter cited as NSF, *National Patterns, 1953–1978-79*).

applied research, industry performed the bulk of the work ($8.2 billion) and was followed by the federal government ($2.6 billion) and the colleges and universities ($1.6 billion).[5]

Development

The historical pattern of development funding mirrors that of applied research funding. The federal government, following a period of predominance, was overtaken during the 1970s by industry. In 1960, out of a total of $9.3 billion spent for development projects in the United States, the federal government provided $6.3 billion and industry $2.9 billion. The gap closed by 1970, when, out of a total outlay of $16.8 billion, the federal government provided $9.3 billion and industry $7.5 billion. Beginning in 1974 and continuing every year since, industry has surpassed the federal government as a source of development funds. In 1980, out of a total of $39.3 billion spent on development projects, industry spent $21.7 billion and the federal government $17.3 billion.

As with applied research, industry has always been the chief performer of development activities. In 1960 industry used $8.1 billion of the $9.3 billion spent on development. In 1980 industry performed development projects totaling $33.2 billion, and the federal government performed development projects totaling only $4.3 billion.[6]

R & D by National Objective

In 1953, 90 percent of federal R & D funding was designated for defense, 9 percent for civilian R & D, and 1 percent for space. Since 1953 there has been a gradual but steady decline (except for a brief Vietnam-related upsurge in the late 1960s) in the percentage of federal funds for defense and a corresponding slow but steady increase in the amount of federal money supporting civilian R & D. Funding for space increased rapidly from 1960 to 1965 because of the Apollo program, but then declined steadily until the mid-1970s, when it stabilized. The overall figures read as follows: in 1960, defense outlays accounted for 80 percent of all federal R & D dollars, with civilian programs making up 15 percent and space 5 percent; in 1965, defense accounted for 50 percent, civilian programs 18 percent, and space 32 percent; in 1970, defense received a total of 57 percent of federal

5. NSF, *National Patterns, 1981*, p. 27.
6. Ibid., p. 28.

FIGURE 1

FEDERAL RESEARCH AND DEVELOPMENT SUPPORT OF SELECTED
BUDGET FUNCTIONS, 1971–1980

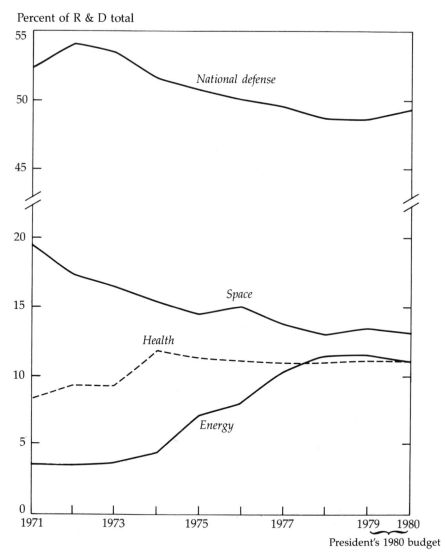

Percent of R & D total

SOURCE: National Science Foundation.

R & D dollars, civilian programs 25 percent, and space 18 percent; in
1975, defense received 53 percent, civilian programs 33 percent, and
space 14 percent; in 1980, defense received 50 percent, civilian pro-

grams 35 percent, and space 15 percent.[7]

In the civilian sector, the largest increases during the 1970s came in energy, health, and general science. Since 1970 R & D expenditures for energy and health have increased from 2 percent and 7 percent, respectively, of the federal R & D total to more than 10 percent each. (See figure 1 for the breakdown of R & D budget trends from 1972 to 1980, by budget function).[8]

R & D in Industry

Industry is currently funding just over half of the nation's R & D activities. During the 1960s, one-half of the funds spent by industry were provided by the federal government. By 1980, however, industry funded about two-thirds of the R & D it performed. The federal percentage dropped because of government cutbacks in space and defense and because of increased industry support for R & D.[9] Its programs are heavily concentrated in applied R & D.

Nearly 80 percent of industry R & D funds are spent by companies in five areas: aircraft, electrical equipment, machinery, motor vehicles, and chemicals. Aircraft and equipment companies make up almost one-half of this percentage.[10]

Even when it is not directly funding areas of R & D, the federal government can have a marked effect on industry expenditures. Thus, since 1975, industry-funded R & D for pollution abatement has risen 11 percent per year in constant dollars as a result of environmental mandates. A similar pattern has emerged in regard to industry energy R & D, where the result has been an increasing emphasis on basic research. From 1975 to 1979, largely as a result of work on energy projects, industry generated a 20 percent increase in funding for basic research.[11]

Academic R & D

Universities and colleges spend just over one-half of all basic research funds in the United States, the federal government providing more

7. Adapted from table B-8 in NSF, *National Patterns, 1953–1978-79*, p. 44.

8. NSF, *National Patterns, 1981*, pp. 10–11.

9. NSF, *National Patterns, 1980*, p. 6; NSF, *National Patterns, 1953–1978-79*, pp. 13–15; see also Willis H. Shapley et al., *Research and Development: AAAS Report III: R & D in the Federal Budget: FY 1979; R & D, Industry and the Economy* (Washington, D.C.: American Association for the Advancement of Science, 1978), pp. 53–71 (hereafter cited as *AAAS Report, 1979*).

10. NSF, *National Patterns, 1980*, p. 6.

11. Ibid.; *AAAS Report, 1979*, pp. 63–64.

FIGURE 2

RESEARCH AND DEVELOPMENT EXPENDITURES AS A PROPORTION OF
GROSS NATIONAL PRODUCT IN SELECTED COUNTRIES, 1967-1979

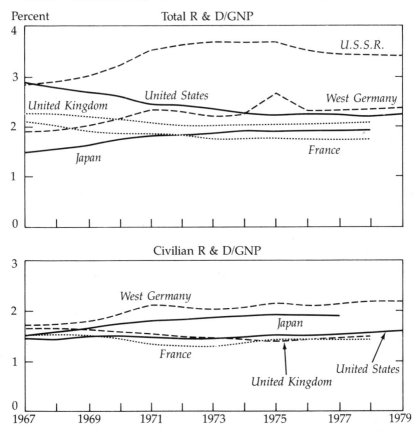

SOURCES: National Science Foundation, Organization for Economic Cooperation and Development, and Robert Campbell (Indiana University).

than two-thirds of them. From 1968 to 1974, academic R & D expenditures in constant dollars either remained about level or slightly declined, but from 1975 to 1980 they increased at rates significantly above inflation. During the 1970s there was also a noticeable shift by universities and colleges away from basic research and toward applied research. Basic research made up 69 percent of all academic R & D expenditures in 1978, compared with 77 percent a decade earlier. The proportion of funds allocated to applied research grew from 19 percent to 26 percent.[12]

Over the past two years, the DOD again has emerged as a significant and rapidly growing supporter of academic research. DOD funding for colleges and universities increased 42 percent from fiscal 1980 to 1982 and reached $645 million in the Reagan fiscal 1982 budget. Given the priorities of the Reagan administration, it is likely that DOD will be an important source of academic R & D funding in the next few years.[13]

International Comparisons

There are two measures of the relative emphasis placed on R & D activities by different countries: the ratio of R & D expenditures to gross national product (GNP) and the number of scientists and engineers in the labor force. In absolute terms—dollars and numbers of scientists and engineers—the United States continues to be far ahead of other countries, but in relative terms, other mature industrial nations since the 1960s have been closing the gap.

Throughout the 1960s the United States devoted almost 3 percent of its GNP to R & D, more than any other country. During the 1970s, however, with the decline in spending for defense and space research, the nation's ratio of R & D to GNP declined while those of other industrial nations increased. In addition, one-half of the R & D funds in the United States were going into defense and space activities. Other Western nations spent only a small amount of their R & D funds on such activities. Thus in 1967 the United States had a civilian R & D–GNP ratio of 1.48 percent; West Germany, 1.70 percent; Japan, 1.52 percent; the United Kingdom, 1.65 percent; and France, 1.50 percent. In 1975, the U.S. ratio was 1.50 percent; West Germany, 2.19 percent; Japan, 1.89 percent; the United Kingdom, 1.39 percent; and France, 1.39 percent. In 1978, the U.S. ratio was 1.54 percent; West Germany, 2.19 percent; Japan, not available; France, 1.35 percent; and the United Kingdom, 1.47 percent. (See figure 2.)[14]

The United States continues to lead other industrial nations in the ratio of scientists and engineers engaged in R & D per 10,000 popula-

12. NSF, *National Patterns, 1981,* p. 26; NSF, *National Patterns, 1980,* pp. 6–7; see also NSF, *Federal Funds, 1979-81,* pp. 18–23.

13. Office of Management and Budget, *Special Analyses: Budget of the United States Government: Fiscal Year 1980* (Washington, D.C., 1980), p. 311; Willis Shapley et al., *Research and Development: AAAS Report VI; New Directions for R & D; Federal Budget—FY 1982; Industry; Defense* (Washington, D.C.: American Association for the Advancement of Science, 1981), pp. 25–26.

14. NSF, *National Patterns, 1981,* p. 30.

FIGURE 3

ANALYSIS OF THE U.S. RESEARCH AND DEVELOPMENT EFFORT, 1981

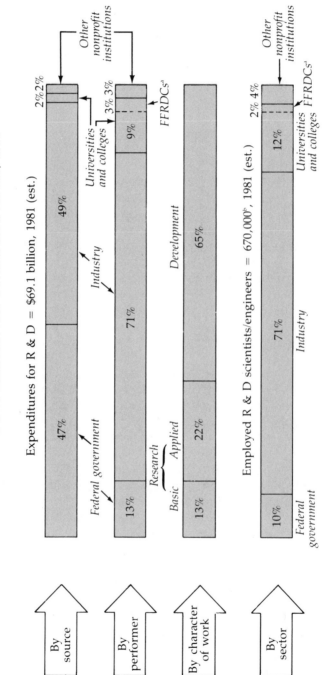

Expenditures for R & D = $69.1 billion, 1981 (est.)

Employed R & D scientists/engineers = 670,000[b], 1981 (est.)

a. Federally funded research and development centers administered by universities and colleges.
b. Full-time equivalents.
SOURCE: National Science Foundation.

FIGURE 4

U.S. RESEARCH AND DEVELOPMENT EXPENDITURES AS A PROPORTION
OF GROSS NATIONAL PRODUCT, 1961–1981

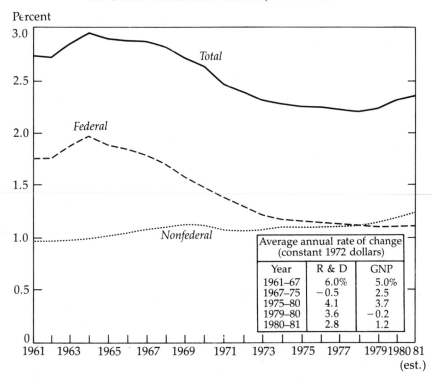

SOURCES: National Science Foundation and Department of Commerce,.

tion, but that ratio has declined since the late 1960s, while those of
other nations have climbed. Thus between 1967 and 1977 the ratio in
the United States declined from 66.1 to 57.7, while in other industrial
nations it increased: West Germany, 24.9 to 44.3; Japan, 27.8 to 49.9;
and France, 25.3 to 30.3. Although precise numbers are difficult to
obtain, it is estimated that over the same ten-year period the Soviet
Union increased its ratio of scientists and engineers per 10,000 population from just over 50 to about 90. (See figures 3 and 4.)[15]

15. Ibid.

Appendix B
The Challenge to Orthodoxy

A number of individuals and organizations that were influential in shaping the Reagan administration's thinking and policy hold views that strike at the very foundations of the rationale for federal support of science and technology. Three voices of dissent and challenge will be examined: the economists Milton Friedman and Simon Rottenberg and a fount of conservative ideas and theories, the Heritage Foundation.

Milton Friedman. The most far-reaching attack on the premises of the federal science support system has been mounted by Milton Friedman. He would do away with public funds not only for applied research and demonstration programs but also for basic research. He has called for the abolition of the National Science Foundation, the National Institutes of Health, and all government aid to higher education.[1]

Friedman bases his recommendations on a combined series of ethical, economic, and political judgments. He holds that the political and bureaucratic process by its nature distorts and corrupts science and misuses and wastes scientists. Friedman says: "The scientific ability of really able people is being diverted from the goals they would like to pursue themselves to the goals devised by government officials." Further, bureaucratic competition operates against support for the best research: "You can't get government support for really innovative projects unless you have a man who is extremely eminent. But if you have some person at the bottom of the academic totem pole, who has some crazy idea, he can't get funded."[2]

He says that government research projects cost much more than projects that are privately funded. Private patrons, he adds, would

1. Nicholas Wade, "Why Government Should Not Fund Science," *Science*, October 3, 1980, p. 33.
2. Ibid.

support research of true worth at less cost if the government withdrew.

More fundamentally, he turns on its head the usual argument for public support of basic research, which is based on the lack of appropriability and the high-risk, serendipitous nature of basic research. The high uncertainty of results, he says, raises a fundamental ethical question in the use of public money:

> What ethical justification do you have for extracting tax money from people for purposes that do not yield them some greater benefit? You have to be able to say that the extra dollar spent on research will produce more than a dollar's worth of benefit to the person from whom the dollar was taken. That is a hard proposition to establish in the case of science.[3]

When queried about how the nation could be certain that enough private capital would be forthcoming in support of research, Friedman replied:

> On whom should the burden of proof be? On those who wish to extract money from the low-income taxpayer, or on those who argue the other way? I challenge you to find a single study justifying the amount of money now being spent on government support of research.[4]

Simon Rottenberg. Simon Rottenberg, an economist at the University of Massachusetts, has written extensively on the political economy of public science. Unlike Friedman but in consonance with most other economists, Rottenberg sees a role for the federal government in funding basic scientific research. In a paper delivered during the December 1980 Public Policy Week at the American Enterprise Institute as the Reagan administration was coming into office, Rottenberg said:

> The only scientific and technological research for which public sector expenditure is clearly indicated is that for which private and social costs and benefits diverge, such as basic research. In that case, the market is imperfect and there will be systematic underinvestment in such research, if the market is permitted to determine how much of it is to be done.[5]

3. Ibid.

4. Ibid.

5. Simon Rottenberg, "Government and Innovation: The Effects of Policy on Science and Technology," in *AEI Public Policy Papers: The 1980 Public Policy Week Papers, with Introductory Essays* (Washington, D.C.: American Enterprise Institute, 1981), p. 192.

Rottenberg, however, holds that NSF and other federal agencies have interpreted definitions of basic research too loosely and that much of what is labeled basic is in reality applied research that the private sector should be funding. He says:

> An active science policy which proceeds on the postulate of science as a public good in the case of basic research must also be employed with care because there are gray areas in which the practical consequences of basic research discoveries might be foreseen. It is not clear in such cases whether the research is clearly and fundamentally basic and hence warrants governmental support, rather than permitting processes of the market to decide whether it should be undertaken and how much resources should be devoted to it.[6]

Rottenberg gives a series of examples of research projects funded by the government that are more appropriate for private support. He mentions projects to advance "basic knowledge in such fields as chemistry, enzymology and plant physiology . . . to understand the mechanisms by which plant and bacteria collect, store and convert or release energy of the sun," which, he says, should be supported by agricultural commodity or energy companies. Projects to study the "chemistry of the nervous system" in order to treat behavioral problems leading to obesity, drug and alcohol abuse, senility, and schizophrenia should be funded by pharmaceutical manufacturing firms. Basic research on new materials such as amorphous semiconductors for electronic device applications, photosensitivity polymers for dry lithography, and substitutes for low-loss transfer cores should be of interest to high-technology firms and their suppliers, according to Rottenberg.[7]

He has reservations about the rigor with which federal agencies define basic research, but he levels his strongest criticism at public support of civilian, nondefense applied research, demonstration, and commercialization projects. Most of these projects, he says, "do not meet the unappropriability [the public goods] standard" and should be abandoned.

Rottenberg cites a number of applied research and demonstration projects as clear-cut examples of "bureaucratic distension" and the operation of public authorities "in areas in which the social judgment of the market would give better results":

The Department of Commerce, for example, wants a new

6. Simon Rottenberg, "The Economy of Science," draft article, p. 13.
7. Ibid., pp. 13–15.

generation of very large cargo carrying tankers to achieve goals of safety, dependability, and productivity. . . . The Department of Health and Human Services wants to find a blocking agent to treat drug overdose victims. The Department of Energy wants research on advanced catalysts for liquefying and gasifying coal. The Department of Transportation wants research on applications of micro-electronics to the automobile, on pipeline corrosion control, on automated systems to improve the circulation of people in city centers, and on the development of materials to replace asphalt concrete and portland cement in highway construction and repair. . . . It would be nice to have all these things if they came at zero cost. They do not. They consume resources that have other uses, so they imply social opportunity costs. . . . They are not public goods. There is no problem of incapacity of investors to capture the whole gain they would produce. There is no problem of exclusion and there would be no free riders. . . . There is no apparent market failure [and] in cases such as these, science policy intervenes mischievously.[8]

Like Friedman, Rottenberg believes that the political and bureaucratic processes inevitably operate to subvert good science. He argues that "the advancement of science and technology by the public sector is vulnerable to political imperatives," with "congressmen and other political figures [staking] out claims for the location of publicly financed scientific activity in their own constituencies." He goes on to say that "idiosyncratic presidential interests" cause major distortions of scientific priorities and that scientists and academics themselves use "a variety of political strategies in their competition with other claimants." In this situation, Rottenberg says, "the process of evaluation and the exercise of judgment become distorted, inappropriate tests are applied, wrong outcomes are generated, the scientific community comes to be governed by wrong standards, and the program of science is diminished."[9]

In place of the currrent highly politicized system of science resource allocation, Rottenberg would substitute direct grants to distinguished individual scientists or block grants to a selected group of universities. The individual scientists and the universities would then make the allocation decisions among disciplines. The universities would also be allowed to consolidate their funds with other institutions and form consortia to fund construction of expansive capital

8. Rottenberg, "Government and Innovation," pp. 187–88.
9. Ibid., pp. 184–86.

facilities. This system, he concludes, would produce more socially optimal outcomes:

> By applying the method of searching out scientists who have merit, as measured by the consensual judgment of the scientific community, and by permitting them to work on problems that rouse their curiosity and are responsive to their sense of what the scientific community considers important, the government will make a stronger contribution to the advancement of science and the progress of knowledge than it would if it attempts the explicit estimation of the relative values of scientific discoveries or if, as now, allocations are often responsive to parochial and political influences.[10]

At the conclusion of his working paper, Rottenberg defined the "central problem confronting public science":

> The central problem confronting public science policy is to avoid central direction. The judgment of policy makers is not better than the judgment of competitive commercial and intellectual markets. If the outcomes that would be generated by those markets are frustrated and dominated by taxes and subsidies, science policy will have done much social mischief.[11]

Heritage Foundation. Early in 1981, as the Reagan administration was taking office, the Heritage Foundation published *Agenda for Progress*, a series of policy-oriented essays on fourteen budget areas and categories. Each essay was separately written, and the unifying theme of each one was, according to the editor, Eugene J. McAllister, an attempt to "display the virtues of a market approach to federal spending." In his introduction to the volume, McAllister said: "Each author inquires, implicitly or explicitly, whether the federal government should engage in the studied activity and, if so, whether current programs are operated in the most efficient matter."[12]

The author of the essay on science, Richard Speier, like Rottenberg, projected a positive role for public funding of basic research. Also like Rottenberg, he raised, however, certain objections about projects supported as basic research and about the role of public officials in research resource allocation. Speier said that "basic research such as the understanding of the behavior of matter or of the

---

10. Rottenberg, "The Economy of Science," pp. 43–44.

11. Rottenberg, "Government and Innovation," p. 193.

12. Eugene J. McAllister, ed., *Agenda for Progress* (Washington, D.C: Heritage Foundation, 1981), p. vii.

processes governing living things cannot effectively be patented, copyrighted or kept secret. . . . This 'non-appropriability of benefits' of basic scientific knowledge has in recent years become the strongest justification for acceptance of a federal role in space and general science."[13]

At the same time, Speier questioned the tendency of the federal government to become "overly involved in the detailed choice of inputs to these [basic research] programs, with consequent inefficiencies." By inputs, Speier meant activities such as manpower training and education programs to produce scientific skills; procurement of facilities and materials, such as preparation of isotopes for use in medical experimentation and treatment; and the construction of a space transportation system to be used for space research and applications. Speier said:

> When the federal government funds manpower training, facilities, materials, or transportation services that may be later used in a research project that may someday produce knowledge, it is intervening far below the output end of the process of producing knowledge. . . . *The federal government is less effective than the market at making complicated low-level investment decisions.*[14]

The decision to develop a space shuttle, Speier said, represents the classic example of federal intervention at too low a level, with the attendant mistakes and misuse of public resources. He devotes several pages to refuting the economic and technical justification of the shuttle and recommends that *"an early item of business for the federal government should be a re-examination of the economics and the institutional arrangements for space transportation."*[15]

Further, he argues that a longer-term solution would entail turning the space transportation business over to the private sector and purchasing space transportation services as necessary for R & D and for national defense. "There is a strong indication that the private sector has both the willingness and resources to continue to improve and to develop space vehicles, as justified by the market."[16]

Again like Rottenberg, Speier believes that there is too much central direction in public science policy and that the federal government should move to share much of the decision making regarding priorities and resource allocation with the private and nonprofit sec-

13. Ibid., p. 66.
14. Ibid., pp. 66, 68, 69.
15. Ibid., pp. 69–73.
16. Ibid., p. 73.

tors. He recommends that the federal government experiment with the creation of research associations (composed of some combination of corporations, trade associations, and universities). They would make the decisions regarding research priorities and share the costs with the government through some kind of automatic funding mechanism.

Finally, Speier says that the government is involved in too much research that will produce results "capturable" by private industry. Therefore, he says, some of it should not have been funded, at least not fully, by the government. He recommended to the Reagan administration that it begin a "review of such programs with consideration given to backing out of them entirely and leaving their funding to the private sector":

> The criterion for such a federal backout should be that the benefits of an innovation are sufficiently appropriable to the firm developing it (through patents, copyrights, trade secrets, or even early entrance into the market) that the private sector has enough incentives to decide whether to invest in the innovation.[17]

Speier asserted that the rigorous application of these criteria would result in a substantial federal backout from NASA programs for aeronautical research and technology.

In a separate essay on energy policy and energy R & D, Randall G. Holcombe, using the market test and approach, also suggested major withdrawals of federal support for a number of high-priority Department of Energy projects. Regarding synthetic fuels, Holcombe said: "There is no justification for supplementing the market to support energy production, and the subsidy to synthetic fuel producers should be eliminated." Similarly, in regard to the Clinch River breeder reactor program, he argued:

> The press of time will allow little opportunity for a thorough study [by the Reagan administration], but it is likely that the project is not an effective investment. A cost-benefit analysis would probably show that R & D money would be better spent to develop the technology of light water resources.[18]

Holcombe applies the same reasoning with the same results to the solar demonstration and energy conservation budgets: "Energy conservation is an area in which governmental activity is difficult to

17. Ibid., pp. 74–79.
18. Ibid., p. 94.

138

justify. Higher prices give every energy user the incentive to conserve. . . . The profit motive provides the right incentives for cost-effective conservation in the private sector." Holcombe says that some money should be spent on basic research for new conservation technologies but most of the development money should be withheld.[19]

19. Ibid., pp. 95–96.

Appendix C

Relative Ranking of Department of Energy Programs by Energy Research Advisory Board

(millions of dollars)

Electric Supply		*Fuel Supply*		*Conservation and Utilization*		*Science and Technology Base*[a]	
Program/FY 1982 Request	Funding	Program/FY 1982 Request	Funding	Program/FY 1982 Request	Funding	Program/FY 1982 Request	Funding
Higher Priority							
						Materials sciences/112.1	More
						Climate and CO_2 research/16.7	More
						Chemical sciences/73.9	More
Commercial nuclear waste/227.6	Same						
						Health/environmental research/170.5	More
						Biological-energy sciences/9.4	More
				Coal combustion/38.8	Same	Nuclear medicine/50.5	Same
Defense nuclear waste/390.0	Same			Building/community systems/28.0	More	High-energy physics/392.7	Same
				Industrial conservation/0.0	More	University research/10.6	More
		Enhanced oil recovery/20.1	Less			Environment and safety/49.6	Same
						Engineering/math/geosciences/32.3	Same
						Nuclear physics/122.9	Same

Medium Priority

Project/budget	Rating	Project/budget	Rating	Project/budget	Rating	Project/budget	Rating
Conventional reactor/68.0	More	Advanced research and environmental control technology/94.5	Same	Transportation conservation/37.0	Same	Nuclear sciences/37.7	Same
Breeder-fuel cycles R & D/26.1	Little less	Enhanced gas recovery/10.2	Less	Solar applications for buildings/84.7	Same		
Centrifuge/64.5[b]	Same						
Liquid metal fast breeder reactor (base program)/387.8	Same	Coal liquefaction/105.2	Less	Heat engines and heat recovery/15.6	Same	Advanced-energy projects/8.2	Same
Solar power technology/19.4	Less			Multisectors conservation/17.5	Same		
Advanced-isotope separation/85.2	Same	Biomass energy/20.5	Same	Fuel cells/28.6	Same		
		Surface-coal gasification/53.4	Less				

Lower Priority

Project/budget	Rating	Project/budget	Rating	Project/budget	Rating	Project/budget	Rating
Magnetic fusion/456.1	Little less	Mining R & D/21.0	Less	Solar applications for industry/44.0	Less	Technology assessments/3.0	Same
Light-water breeder reactor/58.0	Less	In situ oil shale/16.3	Less				
Uranium resources assessment/5.8	Same						
Electric energy/storage systems/47.5	Less						
Hydropower/0	Zero						
Clinch River breeder reactor/254.0	Less						

(Table continues)

141

Appendix C (continued)

Electric Supply		Fuel Supply		Conservation and Utilization		Science and Technology Base[a]	
Program/FY 1982 Request	Funding	Program/FY 1982 Request	Funding	Program/FY 1982 Request	Funding	Program/FY 1982 Request	Funding
Geothermal/46.8	Less						
		Alcohol fuels/10.0	Same				
		In situ coal gasification/8.3	Less				
Magnetohydrodynamics/0.0	Zero						

a. Science and technology base programs and the research, demonstration, and development programs were evaluated by different sets of criteria and are not directly comparable.
b. Excludes $695.8 million for centrifuge plant construction.
SOURCE: U.S. Department of Energy.

A Note on the Book

This book was edited by Gertrude Kaplan of the
Publications Staff of the American Enterprise Institute.
The staff also designed the cover and format, with Pat Taylor.
The figures were drawn by Hördur Karlsson.
The text was set in Palatino, a typeface designed by Hermann Zapf.
Mid-Atlantic Photo Composition, Inc., of Baltimore,
set the type, and Thomson-Shore, Inc.,
of Dexter, Michigan, printed and bound the book,
using Warren's Olde Style paper.